Electoral systems

The process by which representatives are chosen to vote on our behalf – through elections – has come to be accepted as an integral part of most democratic systems. But there are many varieties of electoral system: the single transferrable vote and 'first-past-the-post' are merely two such systems currently in operation.

The issue of whether the rules governing the current electoral process are in need of reform, provokes perennial debate. In this book, Andrew Reeve and Alan Ware attempt to inform this debate by analysing such critical questions as the role an electoral system plays in allocating values in a society, the principles which should be invoked in the analysis of such systems, the significance of the territorial dimension, and the connection between democracy and the electoral process.

These questions are analysed from both a comparative and a theoretical standpoint. The book looks at electoral systems in relation to democratic theory; it examines justifications for some aspects of modern electoral rules, and it links the study of electoral systems to that of voting systems. It compares parliamentary elections with various other kinds of election, and it looks at the differences between British experience and that of other countries.

Andrew Reeve is a political theorist whose work encompasses both contemporary political thought, and the history of political thought. He is Senior Lecturer in the Department of Politics and International Studies at the University of Warwick. **Alan Ware** is a political scientist who specializes in comparative politics, and in the study of political parties. He is a Fellow in Politics at Worcester College, Oxford.

Theory and Practice in British Politics
Series editors: Desmond King, Jeremy Waldron, Alan Ware

This new series bridges the gap between political institutions and political theory as taught in introductory British politics courses. While teachers and students agree that there are important connections between theory and practice in British politics, few textbooks systematically explore these connections. Each book in this series takes a major area or institution and looks at the theoretical issues which it raises. Topics covered include the police, Northern Ireland, Parliament, electoral systems, the law, cities, central government, and many more. No other textbook series offers both a lively and clear introduction to key institutions and an understanding of how theoretical issues arise in the concrete and practical context of politics in Britain. These innovative texts will be essential reading for teachers and beginning students alike.

Other titles in the series

The Law
Jeremy Waldron

Also from Routledge

The Almanac of British Politics (4th edition)
Robert Waller

The Commons Under Scrutiny
Edited by Michael Ryle and Peter Richards

Party Ideology in Britain
Edited by L. Tivey and A. Wright

Electoral Systems

A comparative and theoretical introduction

Andrew Reeve and Alan Ware

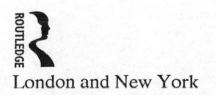

London and New York

First published 1992
by Routledge
11 New Fetter Lane, London EC4P 4EE

Simultaneously published in the USA and Canada by
Routledge
a division of Routledge, Chapman and Hall Inc.
29 West 35th Street, New York, NY 10001

Typeset in Times by
NWL Editorial Services, Langport, Somerset

Printed and bound in Great Britain by
Biddles Ltd, Guildford and King's Lynn

British Library Cataloguing in Publication Data
Reeve, Andrew
    Electoral systems: a comparative and theoretical
    introduction. – (Theory and practice in British politics).
    1. Great Britain.   Electoral systems
    I. Title.   II. Ware, Alan   III. Series
    324.630941

    ISBN 0–415–01204–X
    ISBN 0–415–01205–8 pbk

Library of Congress Cataloging in Publication Data
Reeve, Andrew.
    Electoral systems: a comparative and theoretical introduction /
    Andrew Reeve and Alan Ware.
        p.   cm. – (Theory and practice in British politics)
    Includes bibliographical references and index.
    ISBN 0–415–01204–X. – ISBN 0–415–01205–8 (pbk.)
    1. Elections.   2. Voting.   3. Democracy.
    4. Representative government and representation.
    I. Ware, Alan.   II. Title.   III. Series.
    JF1001.R38   1991
    324.6–dc20
                                                    91–10688
                                                       CIP

Contents

Acknowledgements

We are grateful to the following friends and colleagues for the help and advice which they have given us in the preparation of this book: Jim Bulpitt, John Cunliffe, Desmond S. King, Iain McLean, Carl Slevin, Jeffrey Stanyer, Derek Urwin, and Jeremy Waldron. We are also grateful to the Editors of *The Independent* and The *London Daily Mail* for permission to reproduce short articles from those newspapers.

Andrew Reeve
Alan Ware

1 Introduction

Elections are taking place all the time in Britain. Social clubs elect new members, committees of all kinds elect new chairmen, trade unions elect members to their national councils, and so on. Far less frequently, though, there are general elections to Parliament and to the European Parliament. That we elect our MPs only every four years (or so) is one reason why political scientists recognize that elections are not a very 'intensive' form of political participation. But because we do take part in elections involving other aspects of our lives, the process of electing an MP (and indirectly a government) is not wholly strange and unfamiliar to us. If we reflect on how the various elections in which we have been involved (or about which we have heard) are conducted, it becomes clear that there are a large number of different ways in which elections are actually organized. Consider the following examples.

1 For more than two centuries many gentlemen's clubs in London have elected new members on the following principle. A current member proposes and another member seconds a candidate for membership. Any member who wishes to oppose the election of the candidate may do so by dropping a black ball (anonymously) into an urn before a given deadline. If no-one 'blackballs' him the candidate is duly elected as a member.

2 Every year firms which are limited companies have to present a report to their shareholders at an annual meeting, and it is at this meeting that new members of the board of directors are elected. In fact, the chances that a candidate so presented would not actually be elected are tiny. He or she has already been 'handpicked' by the present directors. They would not choose someone likely to be opposed by the large institutional shareholders. The support of these large institutions is crucial, because in such an election the number of votes you have is determined by how many shares you own. Thus small

shareholders can rarely exercise the sort of veto power available to the club member with his black ball.

3 Many trade unions elect their general councils through a ballot of the membership which invites voters to indicate which candidates they prefer. That is, the members are asked to indicate on their ballot form who is their first choice candidate, who is their second choice candidate and so on. The idea is that, if, say, there are fifteen people to be chosen, the individual voter cannot merely show which fifteen people he or she would like to see elected, but can also indicate an order of preference among those fifteen which is then taken into account in the way the votes are added up.

4 One method of conducting elections which has found favour among some political scientists in recent years utilizes a system of 'approval voting' (see Brams and Fishburn 1978). Suppose we want to elect three representatives to a committee. Under this system voters would be asked to indicate which candidates they 'approve of' (that is, were willing to countenance being elected). The number of 'approvals' for each candidate would then be counted and the three with the greatest number would be duly elected.

Each of the different sets of rules governing how elections are conducted constitutes a separate electoral system. The study of electoral systems, then, is the study of the rules of elections. This book is about electoral systems in Britain, and it is primarily, but not exclusively, about the rules governing the election of political representatives. Unlike many studies of electoral systems, however, it seeks to integrate the analysis of voting systems into the study of electoral systems. Voting, of course, takes place in many contexts other than elections (such as in decision- making by committees), while there are instances of elections in which voting is not employed. Nevertheless, most kinds of elections do involve some form of voting, and we would expect that those who have studied voting procedures could provide important insights for students of electoral systems. That, in general, the study of election rules has not drawn much on recent advances in the analysis of voting systems is a point to which we return shortly. First, though, it is important to stress that studying the rules of an activity is an important subject partly because it helps us to understand the strategic elements of that activity. Consider the following analogy.

If we watch a game of association football, we need to understand its rules in order to have any appreciation of what is happening on the field. However, in addition to understanding the general way in which the game is played (through reading the rule book), our enjoyment of the game is enhanced by knowing how the players try to use their skills and devise a strategy for winning *within the context of those rules*. For example, merely reading and understanding the rules relating to 'offside' will not enable us to understand why some teams drill their back four defenders to operate a very strict 'offside trap' anywhere within their own half, while others do not. To appreciate this, of course, we have to look at the particular range of skills the team's players have, and so on. But our point is that, in part, these tactics are a response by teams to a particular rule in modern football – until recently that in the opponent's half a ball could not be passed to a player unless there were two opponents between him and the goal. Abolishing the offside law would change many aspects of how football is actually played.

To see how the rules of an activity constrain, but also provide opportunities for, particular ways of participating in it is one important way in which it may be studied. While this book is about certain kinds of rules (electoral systems), we focus on the ways in which those rules affect and relate to broader aspects of the British political system. But the book is also broader in scope than the sporting analogy we have just introduced suggests – and this point needs to be considered carefully.

Taking two similar sports (for example, rugby union and rugby league) we would learn a lot from examining how differences in the two sets of rules affect various strategies used in playing the game. Nevertheless, it would make little sense to ask how the different rules facilitate the realization of some more general principle or objective (such as that people become fitter). But in the case of the rules with which we are concerned in this book it is important to consider just such questions. On the one hand, it is appropriate to ask whether one set of electoral rules is more compatible with democracy than another. On the other hand, there is an even 'higher level' issue. Are elections, even ones conducted under the 'most appropriate' rules, the best way of deciding an issue – or might we do better trying to conduct our business in some other way, for example by having a very extensive market system?

Consequently, in this book we are concerned not merely with how electoral systems (and especially the Parliamentary electoral system) work in Britain, but also with important theoretical issues. 'Theory' permeates the book – and in various ways. We raise the question, for example, of how a system of elections compares with other methods of taking decisions. Again, we discuss how an electoral system contributes to the goal of democracy. But theoretical issues are also raised in the context of the operation of the Parliamentary electoral system itself – for example, in looking at the question of how equal the vote is in Britain. We are taking a particular institution – the electoral system –

and examining aspects of it which are significant not just for political scientists but also for political theorists. Before turning to another aspect of the book's focus – that it is about Britain – it is necessary first to say something about electoral systems in general. There are three main points to be made about them in a summary way which are then explained in greater detail.

1 Not only is there a considerable number of electoral systems that we could think of if we tried; in reality there is an infinite variety of electoral systems that could be devised.
2 Electoral systems are key variables in the political process in a democracy, because to a large extent they determine who gets what, when and how.
3 Despite the infinite variety of systems and their importance in allocating values in a society, in most regimes electoral systems tend not to be changed very often or very radically. Particular electoral systems are maintained even when the elites forming the government change.

VARIETY OF ELECTORAL SYSTEMS

If we focus our attention just on those electoral systems used in choosing legislatures, there is a tendency to underestimate the infinite variety of electoral systems that could be devised. Often we might think of plurality electoral systems of the British kind, the Alternative Vote and various forms of proportional representation (PR) as constituting the greater part of a fairly restricted universe. There are three reasons why we are inclined to make this mistake about the range of possible electoral systems.

1 As politics students we are naturally inclined, perhaps, to think of national politics as being the main arena in which electoral systems are used, rather than thinking of their use in small clubs or organizations. Initially, therefore, we might overlook examples like the 'blackballing' procedure mentioned earlier.
2 As a matter of fact, though, the range of electoral systems employed in organizations is relatively small in relation to the range of rules we might find. Organizations tend to copy electoral rules they see working well in other organizations, rather than to spend time devising wholly new systems for themselves – even if those might turn out to be more appropriate. This is largely because most people have a very limited understanding of how electoral systems work, and the strategic possibilities they contain, so that experimentation has been, and continues to be, greatly circumscribed.

3 Research by political scientists on electoral systems, and their constituent elements, has also tended to restrict our focus in a number of ways. Nearly all books about electoral systems define their subject in terms of legislative and governmental elections. In fact, one of the classic studies, Douglas Rae's (1971) *The Political Consequences of Electoral Laws*, defines, an electoral law in this way.[1] Political scientists have been too concerned with either describing different electoral laws for legislative elections or analysing their consequences, rather than with exploring the implications of possible new electoral systems. In saying this, we are not thereby criticizing their work – far from it – but the limited scope of nearly all academic work on electoral systems does contribute to the false belief that there is a limited range of electoral systems that an organization or a state could choose.

But there is another, and arguably more important, point that must be made about the academic study of electoral laws. To a surprising degree it has become divorced from the study of a topic that we might imagine was very closely related to it – the study of voting procedures. Voting is a way of taking a decision (such as to which pub a group of friends should go on a particular evening). Elections also involve making decisions though they can be conducted without counting votes – as in the case of the 'blackballing' procedure. Nevertheless, most electoral systems do employ some form of voting procedure; but, as Dummett (1984: 9) notes,

> there are many features that render the theory of electoral systems far more complex than that of voting on committees. One of them is the dual significance of a vote in a general election under any system which . . . divides the country into local constituencies: a vote goes to determine both who shall represent the constituency and what the composition of Parliament is to be.

In view of the complexity of the theory of electoral systems, we might expect that those who have studied it would have drawn heavily on the work of those who study voting systems. Generally they have not done so. Much of the research on voting procedures in recent decades has been conducted by mathematically-informed economists, whose work is often difficult to understand without an adequate training in mathematics.[2] Consequently, the study of electoral systems has drawn on research on voting procedures only to a limited extent. Dummett (1984: 294–5) himself compared the extensive bibliographies of two important works – one on electoral systems and one on voting procedures – and found that the only writer to appear in both bibliographies was John Stuart Mill!

Divorced from a theoretical underpinning in voting procedures, and concerning itself mainly with well-known electoral systems, much of the discussion has been unnecessarily limited. Certainly, with the notable exception of academic debates about 'approval voting', controversy about electoral systems in Britain has been conducted largely on the issue of 'first-past-the-post' (plurality voting) versus 'PR'. In a sense, the ethos of the Electoral Reform Society is typical. Rather than having an eclectic approach to electoral systems, or helping to devise and popularize new forms of electoral systems, the Society is a fierce advocate of a particular form of proportional representation, the single transferable vote.

Supporters of the present British ('first-past-the-post') system defend it largely because it tends to produce single-party governments. Proponents of PR argue that the present system under-represents important minority views and can give unlimited political power to a party which has a Parliamentary majority based on considerably less than 50 per cent of the popular vote. From much of the debate we might imagine that there were only two main types of possible electoral systems and we must choose either one or the other. But, as we have stressed, there is an infinite variety of electoral systems. It is not at all difficult to think of a system which would reconcile the two views just mentioned. For example, Parliamentary elections might be conducted on a strictly proportional basis so that a party which obtained 42 per cent of the national vote would receive 42 per cent of the seats initially. But, to overcome the objections of the 'first-past-the-post' advocate, we might build in the following additional element. If the party which obtained the largest share of the vote also got more than 45 per cent of the total vote, it would receive an additional number of seats sufficient to give it an overall Parliamentary majority of, say, twenty seats; if none of the parties received as much as 45 per cent of the vote, then there would be no 'topping up' of seats. This electoral system would ensure single-party government when one party had a reasonably high level of voter support, but prevent single parties being able to govern on their own with relatively low levels of voter support.

We must emphasize that we are not advocating such a system ourselves; we are merely showing that there are many more possible electoral systems than usually feature in debates about electoral systems in Britain. As a matter of fact, this particular system was not conjured up out of thin air. It is a variation of a system that was actually used in pre-war Romania, but it is one that no-one seems to have bothered to invoke in contemporary debates about the British electoral system.

THE POWER OF ELECTORAL SYSTEMS

What kind of electoral system is employed plays an important part in determining who or what is chosen in an election, and, beyond that, any policy decisions in which those elected are involved. Electoral systems are not mere details but key causal factors in determining outcomes. Consider again the case of the 'blackballing' procedure in a gentlemen's club and compare that club with one which elects new members on the basis of a vote of all members. (In the latter case a member would be elected if he secured the votes of a plurality of all those voting.) What sort of person would be more likely elected under the 'blackballing' procedure? 'Blackballing' is more likely to lead to the exclusion of someone who is disliked by any one member, and to lead, therefore, to the election of those who are not disliked by anyone – either because they are generally popular or because many members know little about them. 'Blackballing' is an attractive device for social clubs because it seems to promote a harmonious membership, albeit one that is not as heterogeneous as it might be under plurality voting. Amongst would-be members 'blackballing' would promote behaviour outside the club that was not likely to offend any current member – at least behaviour that could be drawn to their attention. Under plurality voting the would-be member does not have to worry so much about the opinion of each individual.

Similarly, at the level of the national political system the electoral system determines important outcomes. It does so directly in that who is elected under one system may not be elected under another system. Almost certainly, for example, if the British general elections of 1979, 1983 and 1987 had been held under the West German type of party list electoral system, the votes cast would have resulted in a minority government or the need for a coalition government; Conservative governments with working Parliamentary majorities would not have been produced. But the particular electoral system also has indirect effects on outcomes. It influences what kinds of parties are formed – in Britain the electoral system works against the formation of new parties, except when they have the potential for a strong base in a particular territory. 'Splintering' of major parties has been limited for this reason too – the formation of the SDP (from a split in the Labour party) in 1981 being one of the rare exceptions. More indirectly still, and because of its differential impact on the parties, the electoral system influences if or when a policy issue gets on to the national political agenda.

Changing the electoral rules can change the 'shape' of electoral politics. This is illustrated well by the reduction in the influence of the

Communist party between the Fourth and Fifth French Republics. During the Fourth Republic (1946–58) the Communists regularly polled about a quarter of the total vote and returned a similar number of deputies to the French Parliament. The existence of this large group opposed to the regime was an important cause of the governmental crises that regime continually faced. Under the electoral rules adopted by the Fifth Republic, it became much more difficult for the Communists to translate their share of the vote into Parliamentary seats. This under-representation of the Communists was one of the factors contributing to the much greater stability of the regime. It would seem then that, if 'changing the rules can change the game', all actors in an electoral system would have a strong incentive to change the electoral rules to their own advantage. As we shall see in the next section, in reality there is less modification of electoral rules – whether at the level of the state or in other bodies – than we might expect, given this apparent power to influence outcomes. Moreover, this power of electoral systems must be placed in context, for we must be careful not to make the false assumption that the rules determine everything; they do not.

Controversy about the impact of electoral rules was at the centre of one of the main debates within political science in the immediate post-war decades – concerning the relevance of sociology to the study of politics. Certainly until the late 1950s, many political scientists (and practising politicians too) believed that you could get the political results you wanted simply by providing the appropriate institutional framework. (The British government in the 1950s seemed to believe that it would create liberal democracy in its ex-colonies in Africa by setting up Parliamentary institutions there; the attempt largely failed.) In relation to electoral politics it was widely accepted that the type of electoral system a country used determined the kind of party system it had. The most famous argument on these lines was made by Maurice Duverger (1954: 217) when he said of an electoral system:

> Its effect can be expressed in the following formula: *the simple-majority single-ballot system favours the two-party system*. Of all the hypotheses that have been defined in this book, this approaches the most nearly perhaps to a true sociological law.
>
> (Italics in original)

One source of opposition to Duverger's claim, and to similar ones about the power of electoral rules, came from those who argued that it neglected the role of social phenomena as determinants of party systems. The growing influence of sociological methods and theories in political science in the 1950s, especially in the United States, fuelled opposition to the view that party systems were essentially the product of electoral systems.

One of the best-known alternative arguments (to those like Duverger's) about the causes of party systems was outlined by Lipset and Rokkan (1967). According to them, party systems were linked to the historical development of four lines of social cleavage – centre–periphery, state–church, land–industry and owner–worker. The main determinants of modern party systems were: which cleavages emerged; when they emerged; and how the conflicts were resolved. Electoral systems modified, but did not fundamentally transform, socially determined party systems.

In more recent years it has become apparent that, while Duverger claimed too much influence for the role of electoral systems, the sociological approach understated their significance. Parties are not merely the product of social forces but of institutional structures as well. For example, the nature of a state bureaucracy in the early stages of the process of democratization affects the patronage opportunities for political parties, and hence influences the kinds of parties that will compete for, and gain access to, public office. But this example itself places the role of electoral systems in perspective, for an electoral system is not the only kind of institutional structure within a state that influences the nature of that country's party system.

Nevertheless, electoral systems should not be thought of as a secondary element of electoral politics. Duverger was surely correct in arguing that plurality voting in a single ballot system (the kind of election used for the British Parliament) does tend to frustrate the development of multi-partyism. Although it is possible that a Parliament dominated by two parties could be maintained in Britain under some form of PR, as the Maltese example of two-partyism under PR indicates, it would be less likely to persist. Changing the rules would change the electoral game. But how much it would change it is difficult to tell. One widely accepted argument among political scientists is that the timing of a switch to PR has a significant bearing on the subsequent development of a party system. Countries which adopted PR soon after the vote was extended to most of the population tended to have highly fragmented party systems – in that voter support was divided between a relatively large number of parties. This came about because there had been no chance for larger parties to cultivate the loyalty of new voters before the introduction of PR. Where PR was introduced significantly later than mass suffrage, party fragmentation tended not to occur because the larger parties had loyal electorates who tended not to desert them *en masse* for new or 'splinter' parties. On this basis we would not expect a fragmented party system to emerge in Britain if PR were introduced here, but of course there are other factors which could still facilitate such a development.

THE CONTINUITY OF ELECTORAL SYSTEMS

We have argued that, in principle, in any organization or political system there are likely to be actors who would increase their own electoral chances or those of their candidates through changing the electoral rules. Consequently, we might expect that debate about these rules would be at the very heart of political controversy – with regular changes in the electoral system as the balance of political forces changed. In practice, and with some exceptions, this is not a pattern of politics that has developed. Beyond some tinkering with the electoral system, organizations and regimes tend not to make changes.

There are some notable exceptions. In the mid 1980s the French Socialist government, which came to power in 1981 for the first time in the Fifth Republic, was fearful of losing its Parliamentary majority at the 1986 elections. To reduce the likelihood of defeat, and certainly a heavy defeat, it changed French electoral law so that the 1986 elections would be contested under a form of PR rather than by the 'run off' method used previously. This did have the effect of reducing the Socialists' losses from what they probably would have been otherwise, but the conservative parties still obtained a Parliamentary majority. In turn, once in office, the conservative parties reversed the Socialists' reform. Again, in 1989 the Greek government successfully changed its electoral system to make it more difficult for its main opponents to obtain a Parliamentary majority; in both of the 1989 general elections the main opposition party failed to win such a majority despite receiving a share of the popular vote that probably would have produced a majority under the old electoral rules. But why are such examples not more common? There are six main reasons for the general persistence of existing electoral systems.

Ignorance

While it is obviously far less true at the level of the state, in many organizations most people are unaware of the possibility of using different electoral systems or of the different effects they might have. What Riker (1986: 142) has said of voting is especially true of elections: 'Most people seem to believe that voting is pretty simple. People cast ballots; someone adds them up; and, presto, there is a straightforward decision. But voting is not at all simple.' It is not only the lesser actors in an organization who fail to understand the strategic implications of electoral rules; many leaders also fail to do so. Even among politicians an understanding of the consequences of different electoral rules is often limited. Usually they have a good intuitive grasp of how the present electoral system works, and how small modifications to it will affect them, but beyond that most do not bother to enquire.

An example of a group of 'elite' politicians not fully understanding the strategic implications of the rules governing an election was the election for the leadership of the Conservative party in 1975. The sole voters were the party's MPs. (An election had been used only once before (in 1965) to select the party leader, and the rules had been modified after the 1974 general election defeats.) Edward Heath submitted himself for re-election, and quite a number of the 130 MPs who voted for his main opponent in the first round of voting (Margaret Thatcher) were doing so merely as a protest against Heath's style of leadership. They did not really want her as leader, but they did not realize that, if a sufficient number of them voted for her, a 'bandwagon effect' would emerge. The 'bandwagon' would be impossible to stop in the second round of voting. Indeed, this is what happened. Mrs Thatcher got so many votes in the first round of voting (though not a majority) that her unenthusiastic supporters found themselves tied in to supporting her again – because she seemed unstoppable now and they did not want to support a losing cause. Had these MPs appreciated the strategic aspects of the particular voting system being used, they may well have acted differently in the first round of voting and Mrs Thatcher would not have become party leader. (By 1990, when Mrs Thatcher herself was challenged for the leadership of the Conservative party, some of the strategic implications of this particular voting system were more widely appreciated by the party's MPs. For example, it was suspected that a failure by the party leader to obtain an outright victory on the first ballot might make Mrs Thatcher's position untenable; indeed, this proved to be the case.)

Another example of electoral rules not being fully understood by politicians concerns the election for the Labour party's Deputy Leadership in 1981. The party's National Executive did not understand how much difference the treatment of abstentions by MPs might make to the overall allocation of votes; they regarded this point as trivial. In fact, under the procedure adopted, Dennis Healey won the election whereas Tony Benn would have won if an alternative procedure advocated by an MP had been used (Dummett 1984: 2–3). If politicians do not understand the implications of existing rules, they understand even less fully the strategic consequences of changing existing rules.

Constitutional constraints

Many organizations and states prevent changes to some (or all) aspects of their electoral systems from being enacted merely by a simple majority of the present incumbents. For example, a majority of the US Congress could not pass legislation of the ordinary kind to allow Congress to be dissolved, and new elections to be held, whenever a majority of the Congress wished to do so. To effect such a change, an amendment to the US Constitution would have to be enacted, and the amendment procedure requires far greater political consensus than other kinds of legislation. When an organization or state has a written constitution it can choose how much (if any) of the existing electoral rules should be protected in this way, and there is considerable variation in this practice. Nevertheless, constitutional constraints are often an important factor restricting changes to existing electoral systems. (When, as in the British case, there is not a written constitution, a majority in the legislature can change the electoral system whenever it wishes to – though it is subject to the political constraints indicated below.)

The beneficiaries are already in office

Usually those best placed to change an electoral system are those who have already been elected under the existing system. Since they have shown they can be elected under it, why should they change it? Of course, there are some circumstances in which this argument does not hold. For example, when a long-disadvantaged opposition finally does get into office, it may well believe that it is unlikely to repeat its success under the existing rules. Nevertheless, there are far more occasions when the incumbent electee believes that he or she is a beneficiary of the existing system. For instance, for decades in Britain the dominant view among the Labour and Conservative party elites was that the existing electoral system at least gave their own parties a chance of winning a Parliamentary majority; under any form of proportional representation they would be likely to have to share power with a third party, something which was thought much less desirable.[3] Generally, then, the existing rules are ones which work to the advantage (at least to some extent) of those most able to change them. It is only when a regime or organization collapses, and has to be reconstructed, or when a long-standing opposition comes to power, that a change in electoral rules becomes likely. Two examples from France illustrate this point.

The electoral rules of the Fifth Republic were not changed until after the Socialists came to office in 1981. The conservative parties which had governed France since 1958 believed that they could preserve a Parliament-ary majority under the existing rules and had no incentive to tamper with them. The Socialists did not move to change the rules either, at least at first, because they had seen in 1981 that they could win a large Parliamentary majority despite them. But as the government became more unpopular, they were increasingly aware of their vulnerability under the existing electoral laws – and it was then that they changed the rules.

When a regime collapses those reconstructing it can start anew and in doing so they can try to rectify the limitations of the fallen regime. In 1946, at the foundation of the Fourth Republic, PR was introduced in an effort to increase the influence of parties in a French political system in which local personalities and local elites dominated. To some extent the reform was successful, but really strong pro-regime parties did not emerge, and the presence of strong anti-regime parties meant that PR contributed to the political instability of the Fourth Republic. When that Republic collapsed in 1958, the authors of the Fifth Republic (Charles de Gaulle and his advisors) deliberately abandoned the use of PR.

The consequences of change are uncertain

Some of the consequences of changing political rules are not, or cannot be, foreseen and may work ultimately to the disadvantage of those who initiated them. There may be 'loopholes' which opponents can exploit, a subsequent change in the electorate (such as the influx of immigrants to Israel in the 1970s) or new issues on the political agenda; all these possibilities reinforce conservative influences among those who might be tempted to change an existing electoral system. They might end up less well placed than before.

The unpredictable consequences of altering electoral rules, especially in the longer term, suggest that the most effective use of changes is in consolidating power in the short term. A good example of this was the adoption of the alternative vote for provincial elections in British Columbia in 1952 and 1953; it was a device for keeping the social democratic Co-operative Commonwealth Federation (CCF) out of office. Divisions within the two major parties in the province (the Liberals and Conservatives) led them to support this solution. However, with the emergence of a new, and successful, anti-socialist party (Social Credit), behind which Liberals and Conservatives could unite at provincial elections, it was possible to abandon the new electoral system. The value of the alternative vote to anti-socialists was that it enabled the CCF to be kept from power at a time when the provincial party system was in flux (Cairns and Wong 1985: 289–94).

Loss of voter support

To the extent that changing the rules is seen as the naked exploitation of political power, it may increase opposition among potential supporters who would be alienated by such tactics or their consequences. Here again the French experience in the 1980s is illustrative. One of the consequences of introducing PR was to allow the National Front to elect a considerable number of deputies in 1986. Their gains contributed to the limitation of Socialist party losses in 1986, but thereafter the Socialists could always be accused of having helped to legitimize the right-wing party. This claim is a major factor constraining the Socialist party from reintroducing PR. Any advantage to be gained from adopting an electoral system more favourable to the Socialists might be offset by the withdrawal of support from those especially worried by the re-emergence of the National Front.

Increasing political conflict

One of the problems of changing rules so as to advantage yourself is that in doing so you may well raise the level of conflict within an organization or a state. Often people get angry if such means are deployed by the victors to increase their chances of winning next time. In some circumstances the consensus which holds an organization or a state together may be thought to be sufficiently fragile that those who would want to change the rules nevertheless refrain from doing so. A fear of provoking a backlash (so that members resign from a club, or citizens resort to violent demonstrations) may well deter reform of the electoral rules.

Together these six factors result in far more stability in electoral rules than might be expected when first considering the significance such rules have. But it is also a mistake to see change in electoral systems as 'unthinkable'. Many countries have altered their electoral systems, and, as we shall see, many aspects of the British Parliamentary electoral system changed as liberal democracy developed. Certainly, there are circumstances in which further reform of that system would become a major issue on the agenda of British politics.

ELECTORAL SYSTEMS IN BRITAIN

We explained earlier that this book is about both the theory and practice of electoral systems; it also focuses on one polity, Britain. But, as will be apparent from the discussion already, we are not confining our discussion to Britain. The reason for this is straightforward. It is possible to understand fully the significance of particular electoral rules, and how they relate to the implementation of democracy, only by comparing them with other electoral rules. Nevertheless, there are limits to the extent to which we can make useful comparisons. Often people ask, as we did earlier – what results would recent British general elections have produced if we had been using the West German system of electoral rules, or, say, the Irish system? There are several reasons why these are difficult questions to answer in any detail. (1) We do not know with absolute confidence how people would have behaved in the voting booth if they were faced with a different set of rules. (2) Even less can we say with confidence what they would have done under voting systems which require or allow them to provide more information about their preferences than the British system does. All we can do is make some assumptions based on opinions about parties revealed in opinion poll surveys.[4] (3) In any case, under a different set of rules (such as ones which make single-party government unlikely) the campaign tactics of the parties would have to be different. Predictions about the electoral outcome are even more uncertain because they depend on predicting this different behaviour as well.

Obviously, using the West German or the Irish voting systems in Britain would change British politics considerably. But exactly how it would change our politics is rather difficult to predict. Simply knowing that it is unlikely that the Conservative party could have secured Parliamentary majorities in 1979, 1983 and 1987 under the West German or Irish systems is not very interesting. If we used those systems so much else about British politics would be different. What we can glean most readily from comparative studies of electoral systems is the general ways in which different systems affect the parameters of politics. In this book we shall try to explain aspects of the British political system by 'unpacking' its electoral rules. In doing so we shall also draw attention, especially in Chapter 2, to examples of elections in Britain which take place outside the political arena. Here too we can place the Parliamentary electoral rules in context by means of comparison.

The remainder of the book is organized in the following way. We begin, in Chapter 2, by asking what an election is, and go on to relate elections to the idea of democracy. We stipulate three conditions that must be met for an elected body to be fully democratic, before going on to compare elections and voting (as means of taking decisions) with the market. In Chapter 3 we examine the historical development of the British electoral system, and then connect it to the three dimensions of democracy we introduced in Chapter 2. In Chapter 3 we relate British electoral practice to three elements of electoral systems – ballot structure, constituency structure and the formula used for translating votes into seats. Important aspects of these elements form the basis for discussion respectively in Chapters 5, 6 and 7. Before looking at these elements in the British context, we return in Chapter 4 to consider again the principle of democracy and the basis of the claim that the British Parliamentary electoral system is democratic. We consider the idea of representation and what is involved in one person representing another. In Chapter 5 we look at a crucial, though often overlooked, concomitant of ballot structure – the secret and 'open' aspects of British elections. Then in Chapter 6 we examine 'constituency structure': the territorial dimension of British electoral politics and the consequences for the British political system of a strongly territorial basis for elections. In Chapter 7 we look at a key aspect of the formula for translating votes into seats – taking the British plurality ('first-past-the-post') electoral system in comparison with some of its main rivals, including some forms of proportional system. Finally, in the concluding chapter we bring together the various strands of argument we have developed and consider briefly their implications for reform of the British electoral system.

2   What is an election?

One of the most famous definitions of politics was provided by Harold
Lasswell (1951). It states that politics is about 'who gets what, when, and
how'. Two aspects of this approach are of immediate interest. First, what
is distinctive about elections as a method of determining the distribution
of goods or values in some collectivity? Secondly, how do different
electoral systems compare in the ways in which they determine these
outcomes? In this chapter we concentrate on the first question. Since
elections are only one possible mechanism by which the preferences of
individuals are translated into outcomes, when is it appropriate to use
an election rather than some other method of generating an outome?
Obviously, we must answer this question before moving on in later
chapters to consider the properties of different electoral systems.

We consider first what, precisely, an election is. Of course, there is
one obvious, and relatively simple, way to begin an examination of what
an election is – to look at a dictionary definition of the term. *The Oxford
English Dictionary* defines an election as: 'The formal choosing of a
person for an office, dignity, or position of any kind; usually by the vote
of a constituent body.' This definition reminds us that people are elected
to the Royal Society, and that non-league football teams used
(sometimes) to be elected into the Football League, just as individuals
are elected to Parliament or on to their parish council. It also reminds
us of the wide range of officeholders who are not elected, of which
hereditary royal families provide the best example. While elections are
always a particular way of taking a decision, the purpose of an election
is not always to choose people who will take decisions. The point of
electing someone to the Royal Society, or electing Wimbledon FC to the
Football League, is not to choose individuals or organizations whose
primary responsibility is to take decisions; to choose someone as a
Fellow of the Royal Society is to acknowledge his or her distinguished
contribution as a scientist, while the purpose of electing Wimbledon to

the Football League was to allow them to play football at the highest levels in England.

Nevertheless, in politics, and in many other fields, the purpose of an election is to choose people who will take certain kinds of decisions, and it is this aspect of elections which forms the main focus of this book. To understand how elections relate to systems of decision-making, we must first outline the six basic ways (or procedures) by which a group or organization might arrange its affairs so that decisions are made. These decisions relate to possible outcomes that the group or organization might face. The six procedures are (1) Contest, (2) Chance, (3) Authoritative determination, (4) Anarchy, (5) Markets and (6) Democracy. All decision-making procedures which are used by groups or organizations are of one of these basic forms, or else combine elements from two or more of these six forms. As we shall see, representative government involves such a combination of methods, each of which must be briefly examined.

METHODS OF DECISION-MAKING

Contest

Let us suppose a local chess club is asked to send one member of its club to a regional championship, and that it is permitted to decide who to send in any way that it wants to. In these circumstances one obvious way of effecting the decision would be to hold a contest in the club, with the winner of that contest being nominated for the regional championship. The point of a contest is to test skills relevant to the activity for which the people are being selected. Consequently, in this example, if we assume that the chess club wants to send its best player, we would expect it to utilize a chess competition as its selection procedure, rather than, say, an arm-wrestling competition. Contests, as decisional procedures, are especially useful when the quality of subsequent actions or decisions is directly related to some skill which is capable of being tested. If we believe that the quality of decision-making by civil servants is affected by the 'calibre' of people recruited to the government service, then setting up a contest which tests the relevant qualities of potential civil servants may be the best method of recruiting them. Indeed, this was the method used for centuries by the state in Imperial China, although it was not employed in Britain until after the Northcote–Trevelyan reforms of 1855.

Chance

Decision-making can be left to chance – to the tossing of a coin, throwing of dice and so on.[1] Deciding by chance is a procedure well suited to three situations: (1) those in which there is absolutely no information available as to what would be a good or a bad decision, (2) those which are referred to in game theory as games where the optimal strategy is a mixed one,[2] and (3) those in which relations between members of the group or organization might be adversely affected by taking the decision in any other way. For example, suppose that the chess club has been invited to send one member on an all-expenses-paid trip to a tournament abroad, and that the tournament is a 'social' event, so that the club does not feel bound to send its best player. There is a considerable benefit available, but one which cannot be distributed among all the members of the club – indeed, only one person can be the beneficiary. In this circumstance, using a lottery would give everyone an opportunity to obtain the benefit. Hence disputes which might otherwise occur, using another decisional procedure by which some individuals might think they have been disadvantaged, would not arise.

Because lotteries are valuable when some benefit or disbenefit cannot be distributed equally among a group, governments sometimes use them to prevent unfairness in a process of distribution. An instance of this was the use of a lottery in the United States after 1969 to determine an order of priority in calling up eighteen year olds for military service. During the Vietnam war many young men had tried to make use of numerous exemptions to avoid conscription, and this favoured middle class (and mainly white) young men. To avoid this bias, the US government changed its procedures for conscription, abolishing many exemptions, and holding a lottery each year to determine the order in which eighteen-year olds would be conscripted. The lottery placed each day of the year in rank order, and the order of conscription was determined by this ranking, with men being conscripted on the basis of their birthdays. Someone with a birthday that happened to have received a low ranking in the lottery might well avoid conscription, because sufficient people might be conscripted before them.

Authoritative determination

A third procedure for ensuring that decisions are taken is to place decision-making power in the hands of one person (or a small group) who makes decisions without reference to anyone else; these decisions are binding. Authoritative determination of an issue is especially advantageous in situations characterized by (1) the need for expertise, which is possessed only by a small number of people, in taking the decision, and (2) the need to take a decision quickly or at small cost. In comparison, for example, with a contest and a lottery, which may take considerable time and other resources to organize, letting a single individual take a decision usually involves relatively small costs. And there are many kinds of decisions which have to be made for which a contest is simply inappropriate, and for which a lottery might produce a poor result. Many decisions by large organizations, including, of course, governments, have to be delegated to officials, because the organization could not function at all if all its members had to be involved with every decision. Much political debate arises, however, both over the extent to which officials (in government, in commercial firms and in trade unions) should be left free to take decisions without consulting those affected by them, and also over the degree of expertise required in taking particular kinds of decisions.

Anarchy

Anarchy is an *absence of rules*, but clearly an absence of rules is compatible with the sort of outcome in which Lasswell (1951) was interested. To say that an outcome was the result of anarchy is not to say (in the way that the term is often used loosely, and misleadingly, in popular discourse) that there was simply confusion or mayhem. Far from it; an anarchistic solution may be efficiently and quickly reached, but the solution is reached without enforceable rules. In a sense, though, anarchy might seem to be the opposite of decision-making because no rules or procedures are used. But the outcome of anarchistic interaction, like the outcome of a contest or authoritative determination, is still a decision in that values have been allocated in the process, and that allocation may well influence subsequent actions by the group. Anarchistic solutions abound in social life – we avoid collisions in corridors in buildings, we queue for buses, and often (though not always!) we can hold conversations without continually interrupting each other.

One form of anarchy is altruistic behaviour – whether that be helping an elderly person across the road, giving money to 'War on Want' or whatever. (Of course, much 'organized altruism' combines anarchy with other kinds of decision-making.) While altruism is certainly a peculiar kind of anarchistic cooperation, we prefer to classify it as an aspect of anarchy, rather than treat it, as some political theorists have done, as a separate type of decision-making mechanism (see, for example, McLean 1987: Chapter 1). While social life would be extremely tedious without anarchistic solutions, many social theorists have disputed the claims of anarchist theorists that all social relations could be arranged on the basis of anarchy.

Markets

Anarchistic solutions often involve informal exchanges – if we are approaching each other down a corridor, and we both move to our left to avoid a collision, then we may think of our actions as involving an exchange, in that both of us are adjusting our behaviour to take account of the other. More obviously, friends and lovers often exchange favours on a highly informal basis, and indeed in a manner that probably they would not like to think of as 'exchange'. In a market, though, exchanges are formalized; buyers and sellers interact to get what they want, and there are rules to prevent people from not fulfilling their part of a bargain. If for no other reason than this, there has to be a state in a market economy to enforce agreements. As with anarchy and authoritative determination, markets are found throughout social interactions, even in socialist and communist states – partly because, like these other decisional mechanisms, they can generate decisions inexpensively. Moreover in many, though (as we shall see later) not all, circumstances markets can make it easier for people to get what they want. If I want to eat an orange (and not an apple) for lunch, and assuming that I do not live in a community which produces them, I can more surely get the orange efficiently and cheaply by buying it in a market than by relying on the other decision-making methods we have discussed. The impossibility of living in a large society without markets for at least some products has been evident to nearly all regimes based on socialism or communism. Today the objection to markets by socialists and communists is to their use in distributing certain *kinds* of goods, for which it is argued there are fairer, or more efficient, means of distribution.

Democracy

The final method of taking decisions is democracy. It is difficult to summarize adequately the difference between democracy and the other procedures, since the idea of democracy is itself controversial (see, for example, the possible accounts reviewed by May 1978). Moreover, because it is an issue to which we return in Chapter 4, we need outline here only the main characteristics of democracy. Our view is that a commitment to democracy is a commitment to political equality. We suggest that, at least in a small group, four conditions have to be met for a process to be democratic.[3] These are as follows:

1 Proposals as to what is to be done can be introduced by any member of the group. That is, every member has an opportunity to get his or her own plans for the group heard by the others.

2 There is discussion about what is to be done on the basis that all can talk about an issue. In part, democratic decision-making involves members coming together at 'general' meetings to discuss issues raised, but democracy is also compatible with high levels of discussion between members away from the formal meetings of the group. However, if there were no meetings at all to which the whole membership went, the democratic process might be weakened to the extent that each member did not get to hear everyone else's point of view.

3 Roughly speaking, members are on an equal footing in being able to participate in the affairs of the group – in relation to time and other resources that might be important in having an input to the club. Democracy requires that inequalities in the distribution of these relevant resources are not so great that the input which different members can make to the decision-making process varies widely.

4 At the end of discussion within the group some procedure is used to decide what the group will do. These procedures could be either informal, involving the emergence of a consensus, or formal, involving the use of voting. Voting procedures provide for a formal way of linking the views, opinions and preferences of members to the policies actually enacted by the group.

Two features of how we have identified democracy here will be apparent immediately to the reader. The first is that democracy in this form could be practised only in a relatively small group – it is what political theorists call 'direct democracy'. Large groups would be unable to utilize this form of democracy because of the impossibility of large numbers of people attending, and taking an active part in, the proceedings of the group. The second point is that democracy entails voting on decisions – just as, the dictionary reminds us, elections usually involve choice by vote. It is not surprising, then, that many democratic theorists have seen elections as a key device in extending democracy from small groups to much larger bodies. By electing a few individuals to represent their opinions and interests, it is argued, a much larger group of people can benefit from the advantage of democracy as a decisional device – that of having an input into the decision-making process. This is 'indirect democracy'. However, electing representatives need not be a substitute for voting on the body's substantive policies. For example, representatives might be required to place all issues on which they will vote before meetings of those who elect them, and then be bound to vote at their own meeting with other representatives in the way that their constituents had mandated them. But electing representatives is necessary if the problems of size are to be overcome at all.

Nevertheless, the election of representatives does not preclude some elements of direct democracy even in very large bodies. On major issues it is possible to hold referendums, in which all those eligible can vote for or against a particular policy proposal. Referendums have been used in many liberal democracies – including the United Kingdom in 1975 on the issue of the country's continued membership of the EEC, and in Scotland and Wales in 1979 on the question of proposals for devolved government to the two nations. Clearly, referendums are not elections, because they do not involve the choosing of persons, but a direct vote on a policy (or constitutional) issue presented to an electorate.[4] They are immediately relevant to students of voting systems but not to students of electoral systems. However, sometimes referendums are of indirect relevance to the latter because they are of use in understanding the impact of some election rules.

ELECTIONS AND NON-DEMOCRATIC DECISION-MAKING

If elections provide a means of making democracy possible in bodies much larger than those which permit direct participation in decision-making, we must also recognize that this is not the only use to which elections may be put. We have already noted that the purpose of electing some people or organizations to a position has nothing to do with their taking decisions in that position – neither the Fellows of the Royal Society nor the clubs in the Football League are the elected representatives of a wider body which requires them to take decisions on its behalf.[5] But there are also many instances in which an election is used to select a decision-maker, but the reason for using an election to do this has little, or nothing, to do with the idea of democracy.

One instance of this concerns the appointment of someone to exercise authoritative determination. There are several ways in which such a person might be appointed. An hereditary principle might be used, as was the case with many monarchies; or he or she might acquire office on the basis of some relevant contest of skill, as in the Arthurian legend; or through a lottery; or possibly the position might be sold, as in the pre-reform British civil service where individuals owned their offices. Finally, an election might be employed to choose individuals for the positions. This can occur when there is no possibility of devising a suitable contest to select the best-qualified persons, while there is a widespread belief that not all candidates will possess the desired qualities for the position, so that it would be unwise to rely on inheritance, chance or purchasing power. Perhaps the best example of an election, in which the electors are supposed to make an 'informed' decision, but where there is no acceptance of the idea that the person elected is in any way beholden to his electors, is that for the papacy. The cardinals who elect a Pope do not mandate him, he is not subject to re-election and he is expected to retain office until death.[6]

But the election of someone to exercise authoritative determination may be justified on other grounds too – namely that an election has symbolic power in legitimizing those in office. This is why non-democratic regimes in the twentieth century have been keen to hold periodic elections even when the result is 'fixed' in advance or when only 'approved' candidates are permitted to stand. However, in Britain too we find many elections which give the illusion of some 'democratic' control but where virtually no power is decentralized to those affected by the decisions of the body concerned. In Chapter 1 we mentioned the example of boards of directors. In nearly all public companies new directors are chosen by existing directors, or imposed on them by very large institutional shareholders. Individual shareholders are usually unable to block such 'elections' or to nominate and elect a candidate of their own. In part, this is because individuals do not have an equal vote as they do under democracy, but, rather, the number of votes they have is determined by the number of shares they own. However, this is not the whole story; if it were, we might expect organizations like building societies to be much more democratic than they are. Building societies give one vote to each person who has an account, but their members can rarely exercise their power. The problem is that the members have no forums in which they meet, so that the cost of mobilizing against the nominees of an existing board is very high, and even highly disgruntled members of a building society will find most of their fellows free-riding.[7] One-person, one-vote is not sufficient to guarantee democratic control if a ruling group can marshal most of the resources behind its candidates. But the very fact that there are 'elections', and not just 'appointments', helps to protect a myth that such institutions are in some sense democratic.

In view of these three advantages that elected offices have (extending democracy, producing 'informed' decisions, and legitimizing institutions), it is not surprising that we find the electoral principle is often fused with a variety of non-democratic procedures in decision-making bodies. Three commonly adopted versions of this are worth mentioning, because they illustrate the point that, even among people who regard themselves as democrats, democracy may not be the only political principle that is built into decision-making structures.

The first example of fusion occurs when elected bodies either have the power to co-opt non-elected members to serve on them, or when non-elected members serve *ex officio*. Many institutions employ these devices because they are a way of bolstering the expertise available to decision-makers. They become incompatible with democracy when non-elected members side with a minority of elected members to overturn the main policies of the majority. (An instance of this in English local government was a vote on the Education Committee of Exeter City Council in 1972, when an appointed member was elected as chairman against the wishes of the ruling majority Conservative group.)[8]

Fusion of procedures is involved, secondly, when elected decision-making bodies use some principle other than a vote to decide who will fill key positions in that body. For example, the body might decide that its longest-serving members will always chair its major committees, irrespective of the wishes of the present members. Such a rule compromises the 'democratic element' of electing members to the body, but may be justified either because it preserves stability in the decision-making process (if there is a high turnover among representatives) or because of the greater expertise of the longer-serving members. The US Congress is often cited as an example of a legislature employing this sort of rule, but it is worth remembering that its use of the 'seniority' principle was never absolute, even before the reforms of the 1970s. Moreover, some state legislatures in the United States actually employ a stricter version of 'seniority' in which even members of the minority party in the chamber have a right to chair a committee if the 'seniority rule' qualifies them to do so.

The last instance of fusion is the so-called 'weighted franchise', in which some voters have more votes than others. Four examples may be given. Before 1948 businessmen and graduates of certain universities could qualify for a second vote in British elections – in the latter case there were separate 'university seats' in Parliament. The present system of electing the leader of the Labour party is based on giving a fixed share of the vote to the Parliamentary party, to the constituency parties and to the trade unions, rather than on one-member, one-vote. The Football League Management Committee gives a vote to each club in the first two divisions, but clubs in the third and fourth divisions may only elect representatives to promote their common interests on the basis of one representative for every eleven clubs. In public companies the number of votes one has is determined by the number of shares one owns.

Sometimes 'weighted franchises' are defended because of the supposedly greater expertise of the voters (as with the 'university seats') and sometimes because of the greater stake some people have in the decisions made by the body. While such franchises are not democratic, they are not always unfair. For example, suppose a group of neighbours gets together to employ someone to cut their lawns; payment to the employee is made directly by each home-owner and is related to the size of his or her lawn; the home-owners elect a small committee to negotiate with the employee the price per square yard of lawn to be paid. Clearly, owners of large lawns have more at stake than owners of small lawns, and it may be thought fair to give more weight to the former's views by giving them more votes in the election for the committee. However, the justification for this kind of weighting becomes much weaker, and the claim for a democratic franchise based on one-member, one-vote becomes stronger, if it is not possible for the small-lawn-owners to form their own group which is not dominated by large-lawn-owners. It is for this reason that, at the level of the state, 'weighted franchises' may be rejected as both undemocratic and, in most circumstances, unfair.[9]

In the real world, then, the use of elections in choosing decision-makers may be for entirely non-democratic reasons, and elections may be used as a way of extending democracy but in conjunction with other devices which weaken or modify the democratic component. Because the existence of elections for members of a group or an organization does not tell us anything about its democratic character, it is often useful to analyse how democratic an elected body actually is. It is to this issue that we now turn.

DEMOCRACY AND ELECTED BODIES

The idea of democracy is controversial, and in a book on electoral systems it is not possible to discuss the various interpretations of the concept of democracy, or the different institutions which have been seen as capable of realizing it. We suggest, though, that many writers on democracy would accept that, for an elected body to be fully democratic, it must meet three conditions. These are (1) that the people electing the body must consist of all those affected directly by the decisions it takes, (2) that the members of the body must be completely accountable to those who elect them, and (3) that all electors must have an equal vote. We examine these conditions in turn.

The size of the electorate

Some writers on democracy, most especially Joseph Schumpeter, have argued that it does not matter how large the electorate is, providing that those who take decisions are subject to re-election by a group of people larger than one they can control directly. On this basis, states such as South Africa and Rhodesia (during its period of UDI) would have to count as democracies. The reason for not accepting this view is that those who are affected directly by a state's decisions (or those of any other body), but are unable to vote against its officeholders in elections, may have no resources with which to express opposition to policies which affect them adversely. This is especially the case since often those who are disenfranchised also lack the economic resources necessary to force the state to take account of them. Having a vote is certainly not a sufficient condition for having influence over an elected body, but in most circumstances it is a necessary one. Many kinds of body have electorates which are co-extensive with the population which is directly affected by their decisions. These include many clubs and associations, and trade unions (see Figure 2.1). In addition there are many more bodies where some people are excluded as voters, but where the vast majority of affected persons do have the vote; among these are the contemporary British and European Parliaments, local councils in Britain, and the boards of directors of building societies. At the other end of the continuum are bodies where the electorate consists of only a small number of affected persons – of which the papacy is an outstanding example.

In between these two extremes are several interesting cases, of which it is worth mentioning three here. The first is the British Parliament before 1928 – the year in which the vote was granted to *all* adult women.[10] (It can be argued that, even then, the British Parliament did not come close to meeting this condition of democracy until the 1960s, because there were still many colonies ruled from Westminster whose inhabitants could not elect MPs.) Another example is the leader of the Conservative party, for which an election was first held in 1975, but with an electorate confined to Conservative MPs. And then there are the boards of directors of public companies, which do not include as voters many people whose interests are directly affected by their decisions – most especially their employees.

The degree of accountability to the electors

If it is sometimes not easy to determine whose interests are affected directly by the policies of a particular group or institution, it is also

High

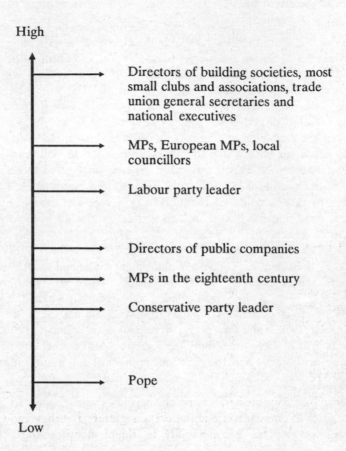

Directors of building societies, most
small clubs and associations, trade
union general secretaries and
national executives

MPs, European MPs, local
councillors

Labour party leader

Directors of public companies

MPs in the eighteenth century

Conservative party leader

Pope

Low

Figure 2.1   Size of electorate in relation to all directly affected persons

difficult comparing different institutions with respect to the level of
accountability they have to their electors. For example, institutions
which are required to have annual meetings to explain policies to those
who elect them may provide innumerable advantages to the officeholders in controlling the agendas of such meetings, while bodies
without formal requirements for such meetings may still be highly
responsive to the views of their electorates. Furthermore, there is the
problem which those who study the concept of power often refer to as
the 'rule of anticipated reactions'.[11] Suppose many members of an
organization have demanded a policy which their elected

representatives have not yet adopted, but the latter now agree to this policy. Have they anticipated the power of their voters to impose it upon them (or to make life difficult for them if they do not), or have they decided independently that the policy would now be beneficial for their organization? In many instances it may be hard to establish exactly why the policy was adopted, especially if some elected representatives seem more likely to have been swayed by the power of the voters, while others give the appearance of making independent judgements. From such cases, it may not be easy to tell just how accountable the leaders are to those they lead.

Nevertheless, by looking at the formal opportunities electors have for removing their representatives (especially through a re-election process), at the resources available at elections to those opposing those currently in power, and at the extent to which representatives meet collectively with those who elect them and feel bound by the decisions of such meetings, we can gauge approximately the level of account-ability. At one end of this continuum we find many local clubs and associations (see Figure 2.2). Because they are small and their members are not dispersed geographically, it is relatively easy for regular meetings to be held between members and representatives; in these sorts of groups too there is usually not a great gap between elector and representative in the level of expertise, so that electors can more readily instruct those they elect as to what they should do in office. At the opposite end of the continuum there is no formal accountability to the electors. Sometimes, as in the case of the papacy, this is accepted by both sides; once they have elected a Pope, the cardinals would expect to have opportunities to persuade him about certain matters, but they know his role does not involve accountability to them. Between these two extremes, the process of accountability is complex and difficult to represent on a single continuum. Let us consider several cases.

Until the 1980s many general secretaries of trade unions were not required to submit themselves for re-election, but their powers were usually limited because union decisions were made by national executive committees which were subject to regular re-election. On the other hand, while the directors of public companies have to meet annually with their shareholders, accountability is often low. This is partly because of the inequality of the vote, but more important is the very high cost of shareholders' coming together before an annual meeting to organize a campaign. Shareholders do not even know who their fellow shareholders are. This is a problem too with building societies. While there are difficulties in dissidents mobilizing opposition in trade unions, the very fact that the branches are required to meet regularly, and that,

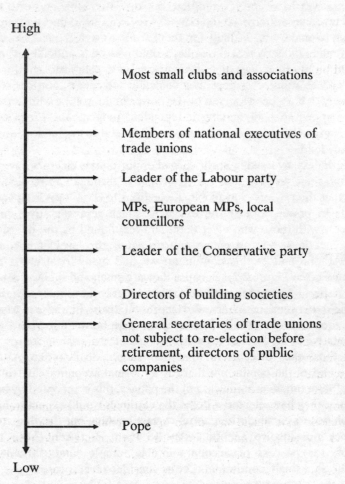

High

Most small clubs and associations

Members of national executives of trade unions

Leader of the Labour party

MPs, European MPs, local councillors

Leader of the Conservative party

Directors of building societies

General secretaries of trade unions not subject to re-election before retirement, directors of public companies

Pope

Low

Figure 2.2   Degree of accountability of officeholders to their electorates

broadly speaking, members will know who their fellows are, provides an opportunity for galvanizing opposition to elected representatives that is largely absent in public companies and building societies. Or consider the accountability of the leaders of the Labour and Conservative parties to those who elect them. In both cases the opportunities for organizing opposition to the leader are greater than the opportunities to oppose the directors of public companies. But while, in theory, the Labour party leader faces greater accountability, because of a requirement that he submit himself to re-election regularly, in practice Conservative MPs are much less tolerant of electoral or policy failure by their leader than are those who elect the Labour leader. Even before the introduction of a formal election of the Conservative leader, 'failed' leaders would quit or would be 'pushed'. Finally, what of the accountability of MPs (in the British and European Parliaments) and local councillors to those who elect them? Here too there is considerable variation, but few of these representatives match up to the democratic ideal of frequent consultation with those who elect them. In part the size of political units prevents this – in anything larger than parish councils, it would be impossible to have meetings which all constituents could attend. But, in any case, many of these representatives, though not all Labour members, have accepted the argument made by Edmund Burke in the eighteenth century that electors should not be able to mandate those they elect.[12]

The degree of equality in the vote

As we have noted, devices such as weighted franchises, the use of co-opted and *ex officio* membership, and devices which constrain how representatives can organize their decision-making in an elected body all reduce the democratic character of an election. Of the institutions we have discussed already, public companies weight voting rights on the basis of the number of shares held, the Labour party employs a weighted franchise in the election for its leader and in the composition of its National Executive (see Figure 2.3), the Football League gives greater voting power to first and second division clubs, and some committees of local councils have made use of co-opted membership. Before 1948 there was a weighted franchise in British Parliamentary elections – a weighting that was actually quite significant before 1918. However, while these devices are undemocratic, because they depart from the democratic principle of equal weighting for each person's vote, we must also recognize that unequal weighting can sometimes actually promote one of the other conditions of democracy. For example, it is possible to imagine circumstances in which a 'weighted franchise' might increase accountability to electors – if those given 'weightier' votes are more likely to demand that representatives respond to the views of those who elect them. Frequently, though, 'fancy franchises' are used to advantage further those who already have the best opportunities for exercising influence – this was the case with the nineteenth-century Parliamentary reforms which granted additional votes for some university graduates and for those owning businesses in constituencies other than the one in which they resided.

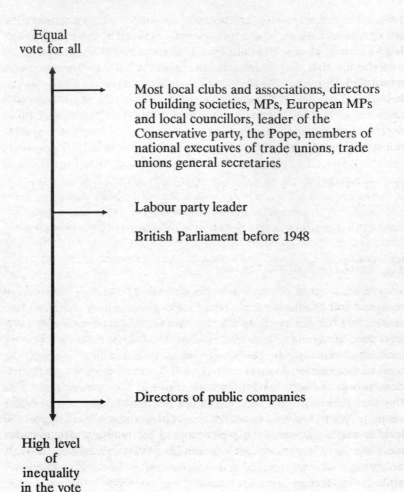

Equal
vote for all

Most local clubs and associations, directors
of building societies, MPs, European MPs
and local councillors, leader of the
Conservative party, the Pope, members of
national executives of trade unions, trade
unions general secretaries

Labour party leader

British Parliament before 1948

Directors of public companies

High level
of
inequality
in the vote

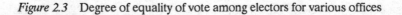

Figure 2.3   Degree of equality of vote among electors for various offices

It is apparent, then, that many institutions which employ elections to
place people into decision-making positions are, at best, only partially
democratic. Nor should we find this surprising. In the first place, as we
have seen, elections may have advantages even for those who reject
democracy as a principle, or who regard it as inappropriate in choosing
particular kinds of decision-makers. Secondly, even today the
democratic ethos has not extended as far as the rhetoric of democracy.

If it is unfashionable in the late twentieth century to describe oneself as anti-democratic, there is still not a widespread realization of the fact that to be a democrat means to accept the decentralization of power – even though that may mean changing many institutions as they are constituted presently. Thirdly, most committed democrats acknowledge that there are many circumstances in which taking a decision democratically, or organizing a body on democratic lines, may impose huge costs on those affected by a decision – costs which a democrat may well consider outweigh the advantages democracy yields.

ELECTIONS AND VOTING VERSUS MARKETS: MARKET FAILURE

However, in spite of the fact that, in many of the most significant social, economic and political institutions, elections are only partly a democratic device, some writers on politics have chosen to interpret them as if they were nothing but this. Primarily these writers are economists, or political scientists who have been much influenced by economic theory, and they are part of a new 'discipline' called *public choice*; this has been identified by one of its practitioners as 'the economic study of nonmarket decision making, or simply the application of economics to political science' (Mueller 1979: 1). This particular definition is more than a little misleading, since there are some forms of 'nonmarket decision making', especially contests, for which it is difficult to see how the methods of economics could be made relevant. What really concern public choice theorists are forms of decision-making in which the preferences of the decision-makers come into play, for it is persons' preferences (and their satisfaction through exchange) which form the subject of economics. Economics might be applied, therefore, to aspects of anarchy and democracy.

Among public choice theorists the greatest interest has been shown in those aspects of political activity which involve democracy – particularly the expression of preferences through voting. They argue that it is possible to compare, say, the outcomes of a small body which votes on the policies it is to enact with the outcomes that might have emerged through a market system. They acknowledge, though, that this becomes less possible with larger bodies, which have elected representatives who vote on policy alternatives, because the connection between the individual elector's preferences and policy outcomes is far more indirect. In particular, as we have noted, many representative systems are only partly democratic in character, and many of their participants want them to retain this quality. Nevertheless, it is still instructive to ask how a system of wholly responsive elected representatives, who voted on policy matters, would differ from a 'minimal' state in which all decisions were effected through a market. In doing this we can understand, and compare, the limitations of exercising choice through voting with those evident in exercising it through a market.

Markets allow a person to get what he or she wants, subject to the constraint imposed by the size of their income. In a perfect economy, therefore, any failure by individuals to get what they want can be put down to their not working out fully what they do want, or not being sufficiently careful when interacting in the market. (However, even those who advocate that all social life should be organized around markets recognize the need for a state; only a state can both enforce contracts which have been freely entered into in the market and prevent actions by individuals which would undermine the operation of markets.) Yet it has long been recognized that an entirely market-based society could not operate in quite this way. To understand this, it is necessary to distinguish between those failures within markets that could, in theory at least, be rectified within a minimal state and those which would require far more extensive state intervention. For our purposes, in comparing the allocation of goods through markets with allocations involving voting, it is the latter which are of much greater interest. Nevertheless, it is worthwhile mentioning the three main problems of markets which might be solved by a minimal state.

One of these problems is the tendency for competitive markets to degenerate into monopoly (control by one supplier of goods) or monopsony (control by one purchaser). Under such conditions the market power at the disposal of a single agent enables it to allocate goods in a way that is both to its own advantage and inefficient. In theory, a minimal state could enact anti-monopoly legislation to prevent such concentrations of market power developing. In practice, of course, controlling monopolistic tendencies is far more complex than this, because the real world does not consist of perfectly competitive markets, but a whole range of imperfectly competitive ones. With imperfect competition, greater concentrations of supply in the hands of a few producers does not always result in greater inefficiencies in allocation. Furthermore, some goods, such as electricity supply lines, constitute 'natural' monopolies, in that the availability of competing sources of supply would itself be wasteful.[13]

The second problem which, in theory, could be solved by a minimal state is that of so-called 'contract failure'.[14] The idea behind this is that some goods which people want are either complex services, the quality of which is always difficult to evaluate, or else they are to be consumed by people other than those who pay for them. With such goods purchasers are at a considerable disadvantage in relation to the supplier, because they cannot easily establish whether the product quality they believe they are paying for is actually supplied. An advocate of a minimal state might argue, though, that if purchasers are really concerned about this, a market in information relevant to such goods would become established, so that concerned purchasers would be able to choose with less risk. Once again, of course, doubts may be raised as to whether in the real world such comprehensive markets in information would be set up.

Finally, there is the problem of the externalization of costs. A large factory which pollutes the air and water of those people who live close to it is, in effect, imposing costs on them, just as smokers in a public place impose costs (in terms of smelly air and health hazards) on non-smokers. In engaging in their market activity, the owners of the factory are transferring costs from themselves to other people. One way of dealing with this would be for the state to require the factory to control its emission of noxious substances. But advocates of a minimal state usually argue that, providing that there are laws requiring those who externalize their costs to compensate those who are affected, state intervention is unnecessary. The problem of externalization can be left to the individuals concerned. Whether, in practice, the costs of legal action, and so on, would prove to be overwhelmingly disadvantageous to the victims of those people and organizations who do externalize their costs is a matter much contested between supporters and opponents of the minimal state.

Our concern in the rest of this chapter is with market failure for which there is no solution compatible with a minimal state.

Distribution of resources

In a market system, resources are allocated on the basis of transactions between individuals; bad deals for the individual can severely diminish his or her resources. As a result, people may be pauperized and completely unable to satisfy any of their wants, and the market itself can do nothing about this. Moreover, not only are those who took the decisions affected, but so too are their families. An entirely market-based society is unattractive because the market would not merely disadvantage individuals (children) who have had no opportunities to make any choices in a market, but it could lead to the extinction of large numbers of people. Proponents of the minimal state have usually sought a remedy for this in one form of anarchy, namely altruism, rather than by invoking the state to correct gross imbalances in the distribution of resources generated by the market. However, except in small communities, the success of altruism by itself, in keeping all individuals even above the starvation level, is modest. The larger the community, the more likely potential donors are to be unaware of the needs of those affected adversely by the market system, and the more likely they are to 'free-ride' (and let others contribute to the 'victims' of the market).

Marginal areas of the economy

Even if the distribution of resources in a society did allow everyone to support themselves, there may be goods or services which some (and possibly many) individuals want but for which they lack the resources to pay. In such conditions, where the ability to pay is limited or uncertain, it may not be worthwhile for suppliers to enter the market. They may not be able to realize normal profits, because, for the goods to be supplied at all on a profitable basis, a certain level of demand may have to be maintained. Where such goods are highly valued, but cannot be supplied by the market, only the state or altruism can ensure that some supply is made available. In the early-modern western state health care and education for most people was supplied (when it was supplied at all) on the basis of altruism. The wealthy gave money to found hospitals and schools, for example. A modern example of a marginal area of the economy is the village shop; the decline in employment in agriculture, and the availability of private transport to those who have moved into country villages, has made many village shops unviable. Yet, in many places, there is still a significant minority of people who are severely inconvenienced by the absence of such shops. Since the state does not subsidize them, and they are not charitable under English law, the demand for them goes unsatisfied.

The undersupply of public goods

Even if markets are efficient at supplying private goods, they are much less capable of ensuring the supply of public goods. A public good is something the supply of which cannot be restricted to those who have contributed towards paying for it. National defence, public parks, and the eradication of an infectious disease are all examples of public goods. Some public goods are supplied by individuals; if I own a historic and architecturally interesting house, which I restore from a derelict state, I may be unintentionally providing a public good: passers-by who enjoy such buildings will have the pleasure of seeing it. My reason for restoring it may have nothing to do with their pleasure, but, nevertheless, something other people want has been created.

In many circumstances, though, there is no incentive for individuals to supply a public good on their own or to contribute towards its supply. This is the so-called 'Olson problem'. When a large number of contributors are required for a good to be produced, the market-oriented individual will reason as follows:

> The chances that my contribution will make the difference between the good being supplied or not are small. If I contribute, and there are insufficient contributors, my contribution has been wasted. If I contribute when the good would have been supplied anyway, because of the contributions of others, I would have done better not to have contributed.

Because of this, there will be a tendency for people to free-ride, and the number of public goods which will be supplied in a purely market economy is much smaller than the number for which there is a demand. Many people would be prepared to pay for such goods, but the market does not provide a mechanism to prevent free-riding by most of them. Only the state can provide such a mechanism.

The tyranny of small decision-making

Related to the problem of the undersupply of public goods is another aspect of collective action in markets – the tyranny of small decision-making. In a market individual consumers can choose only what producers offer to them. What many consumers may want is something that individual producers are not in a position to offer. Consider the following example. Over the last few years specialist ironmongers have gone out of business in many English towns. On many standard items their prices were undercut by new DIY stores, and customers tended to patronize them only for the specialist items which DIY stores would not carry, because turnover of such items was relatively low. Observing this change, many customers faced a dilemma. They would want at least one old-fashioned ironmonger to remain in business, because otherwise they would have no local shop from which to obtain specialist items. They would even be prepared to buy some other items from an ironmonger (and pay more for them) if this would increase the likelihood of one ironmonger remaining in business. But their patronage alone would not ensure an ironmonger did stay open, and they had no means of cooperating with others to ensure that one ironmonger received sufficient patronage. Consequently, such customers behaved in two ways which were fatal for the continuation of a specialist ironmonger. When there were only two or three iron-mongers left in business in a town, not all customers would use the same one, so that the financial situation of all of them continued to worsen. Moreover, because they could not be sure there were other people who felt the same way as they did, those customers who would be prepared to pay more for some standard items tended to 'free-ride' and to 'exit' to the DIY stores. As a result of a whole series of small decisions, which, because of each individual's inability to coordinate with the decisions of others, were rational decisions, the consumers produced an outcome none of them wanted. They were 'tyrannized' by their own small decisions in the market.[15]

The problem of the tyranny of small decision-making is often related to the problem of marginal areas of an economy; in our example it is related in the following way. Ironmongers were prepared to cross-subsidize the holding of a large number of specialist items through the profits they generated on standard items; that is, they would cross-subsidize a marginal area of the economy, so long as, overall, they received a reasonable rate of profit. Cross-subsidization was not contemplated by the profit-maximizing DIY stores, and consumers were never faced directly, therefore, with the option many of them really wanted, which was paying more for some items so that other items would remain readily available should they want them. It is an example of how an outcome could have been different, and conformed more to what people wanted, if the decision could have been taken collectively and not on an individual basis. A crucial limitation of markets is that the very decentralization of the decision-making process can prevent people from getting what they most want.

ELECTIONS AND VOTING VERSUS MARKETS: PROBLEMS WITH VOTING PROCEDURES

It is clear that, with the four aspects of market failure we have considered, outcomes which were 'better' might have resulted if there were an activist state which could take some decisions out of the market. But if the market can be defective, may not collective decisions based on voting by those affected also be flawed? (It should be recalled that we are assuming a decision-making body in which the representatives are completely responsive to the opinions of their electors; but like any directly democratic body, the representatives must use votes in order to decide contested issues.) Indeed, critics of voting argue that there are four related problems in utilizing voting procedures when taking decisions.

Intensity of preference

In a market the purchaser can always show how much more he wants X rather than Y by buying more of it. Usually in voting there is no means by which a person can do this directly – normally, at most, the voter can show that he or she prefers X to Y, and Y to Z. And in some voting systems, it may be possible for the voter to show only that he or she prefers X to Y and Z. In other words, a voter can usually indicate only an order of preference – he or she can give an ordinal ranking of the alternatives available, but he or she has no means of attaching cardinal values to his or her preferences. Now in some circumstances it is possible for a decision-making body to copy the market in allowing cardinal values to be expressed. For example, suppose a committee knows that six substantive issues are to be voted on at a meeting. It could allocate each member fifty votes and allow them to 'spend' as many of these votes as they wanted on any of the six ballots. A person who vehemently opposed one proposal could 'spend', if so-minded, all fifty votes on that one ballot; obviously, this would mean the voter would have no influence whatsoever on any of the other five ballots. Unfortunately, this 'solution' to the alleged inadequacy of voting is not quite so desirable as it might appear at first glance.

One objection to it is that it does not actually remove the other problems with voting which we will consider shortly – they would still be evident in some form even if voters could show intensity of preference in voting. But, in any case, this system of voting would pose a problem for voters in electing representatives, a problem which consumers in a market do not face. Suppose at a general election all voters in Britain were given five votes, which they could divide as they liked between any of the candidates in their own constituency. Let us say that a particular voter overwhelmingly prefers the Labour party to the Liberal Democrats and the Conservatives, but that in comparing the latter two parties the voter has a slight preference for the Liberal Democrats. How should the votes be 'spent'? The voter could give four votes to the Labour candidate and one to the Liberal Democrat candidate, but in doing this, of course, she is depriving the Labour candidate of one vote which might just be crucial for him or her. But if the voter tries to reveal something more like her true preference, which might involve giving all five votes to the Labour candidate, she is not able to show a slight preference for the Liberal Democrat over the Conservative. This is not a problem in a market; if you don't want something you don't have to spend any money on it at all, because you lose nothing by showing which of two unwanted products you prefer. But in taking a collective decision, vital information might not be revealed by a failure to display a preference between undesirable alternatives, and in failing to express this preference a person may end up with their least favoured alternative being chosen collectively.

Moreover, in a committee which uses the usual British procedures of proposing and amending motions, it may be very difficult to know how to 'spend' votes. It is often impossible to know how crucial a particular amendment to a proposal is likely to be and, therefore, how many votes it would be worth expending. Unlike consumers, voters who could express intensity of preference in the way we have indicated would have impossibly difficult calculations to make each time they voted as to how many votes it was worth expending. But, in any case, it can be argued that it is not always desirable in other aspects of social life for people to show how much they prefer one outcome to another, because what they are doing is making *judgements* and not expressing *preferences* (see Jones 1988). This, again, does not apply to decisions in the market. Consider a decision made by the members of a jury. They are supposed to reach a collective judgement as to whether a person is guilty or not. Once the jurors have fully discussed the evidence, and their interpretation of it, it is not relevant that one juror feels very strongly that the accused person is innocent, while the rest feel only moderately strongly that he is innocent; the intensity of their feelings (either way) should have no bearing on the formal decision-making process. What matters is the judgements of each of the jurors, not the intensity of their feelings about their own judgements. It can be argued that in many areas of social life, and certainly in politics, decisions often relate to matters of judgement as much as to issues where intensity of feeling is relevant. (In the political sphere the proper legal status of abortion is such an issue.) Consequently, even if it were possible to take account of 'intensities' in voting, in many bodies it would be inappropriate to try to copy market procedures in this way because there is no value whatsoever in taking account of how strongly people feel about their judgements.

Indeterminacy

In taking a collective decision, a group of voters may fail to produce a uniquely 'best' outcome. This occurs when there are more than two alternatives between which voters can choose. Consider the following case, where the three voters have a different order of preference between the three candidates on which they are voting.

	Voter 1	Voter 2	Voter 3
1st choice	X	Y	Z
2nd choice	Y	Z	X
3rd choice	Z	X	Y

In this example, one majority prefers X to Y, another majority prefers Y to Z, and yet a third majority prefers Z to X. No voting procedure can produce a uniquely 'best' outcome, because there is no such best outcome. Given the preferences the voters happen to have, either we must resort to some other decision-making procedure (such as chance or authoritative determination) or we must accept that in this sort of case the decisional outcome will depend on the particular rules of voting used. For example, suppose the voting rules say that when there are more than two candidates, there will first be an election between the candidates whose names come first alphabetically, that there will then be a subsequent election between the winning candidate and the candidate whose name comes next in the alphabetical list, and so on. In the example shown above, X would defeat Y, but would lose in the subsequent election to Z, but this result is produced entirely by the election rules themselves.

While some voting procedures are better than others in not generating paradoxes, there are some sets of preferences, as we have just seen, which even the procedures devised by Condorcet and Borda cannot deal with adequately.[16] The problem does not lie in the absence of cardinal values in the preferences expressed, though that might reduce the incidence of 'indeterminate' solutions, but rather the problem is inherent in collective decision-making itself. The very act of taking decisions collectively raises problems of aggregation which are avoided if decision-making is decentralized to the individual acting in a market.

The strategic expression of preferences

Voting can permit some people to gain an advantage by not voting sincerely, that is by not voting for their most preferred alternative. For example, consider again the case we have just looked at – a multi-stage election based on the alphabetical ordering of the candidates' names. Candidate Z won that election, but Voter 1 could have obtained a better result by voting for Y, rather than X, at the first election, because Y would then have won that election and would have gone on to defeat Z in the second election. If he or she had done that, Voter 1 would have ensured that Voter 3 obtained a much worse result as far as the latter was concerned. It is important to realize, though, that the strategic expression of preferences can occur in real-world markets. Consider the following case.

Suppose promoters have arranged two Bruce Springsteen concerts in London, one on a Saturday and one on a Monday. Tickets are to be allocated on a 'first-come, first-served' basis by post, but to cut down administrative costs multiple applications by individuals are prohibited, and people can apply only for one concert or the other. (We must suppose that this last requirement can be enforced.) Suppose one group of fans would prefer to go to the Saturday concert, but they believe that demand for the Monday concert will be less. They may well decide to apply for tickets for the Monday concert in order to increase their chances of getting some. By acting in this way they are also decreasing the likelihood that those who really want to go to the Monday concert will be able to buy tickets. In this example, the ability of the fans to get what they want depends on the behaviour of other people, because the promoters have not utilized the 'standard' market approach of setting a price for tickets at which they will just sell all the tickets they have. They are anticipating that the price they set will be much lower, and will generate excess demand, and, most important, in doing this they have linked the supply of one product (Saturday's tickets) to that of another (Monday's tickets). Because customers cannot apply for both concerts, their best strategy for getting what they want is linked, at least partly, to what they think other people will do. It is this connection of the market for one good to that of another which provides for the similarity between some markets and collective decision-making through voting. An unusual condition in markets, though, is a central feature of voting.

The non-optimal supply of public goods

As we saw earlier, in a market-dominated society with a minimal state, there is likely to be a serious undersupply of public goods. By centralizing decision-making, individuals can ensure that a greater number of such goods are supplied. But not all public goods for which there is at least some demand will be supplied. Let us assume that the members of the decision-making body have disparate opinions about public goods, ranging from those who want hardly any supplied to those who want a great number. Assuming the committee uses the principle of majority rule in taking decisions, the quantity of public goods actually supplied is likely to reflect the opinion of the median member of the body – the person who makes the difference between a proposal passing and it being defeated. A significant minority of members may want more public goods than those actually supplied, but they will be unable to mobilize the necessary support to get proposals for them passed. In other words, just as there will be some members who will find that agreed policy provides for more public goods than they want, so there will be others for whom there are insufficient public goods. In this sense, voting cannot do what a market can do (in theory) – namely, give people the quantities of the various goods that they want. For this reason, even those who argue in favour of decision-making through voting, in order to correct the limitations of the market, also often support opportunities for the provision of additional public goods on an anarchistic basis.

From this brief comparison of markets and voting as systems of allocation, it should be apparent that there are major limitations to both of them. Decision-making based on voting (by people directly or by their elected representatives) cannot replicate the market, but neither would it be of much value if it did, since the latter has several important flaws as a means of distributing values in a society.

In this chapter we have been concerned with alternative methods for arriving at social outcomes. In particular, we have focused on decision-making in a democracy; we have seen that, in anything other than a small group, the election of representatives is necessary if everyone is to have an input into the generation of social outcomes. We have argued that there are three elements which determine how democratic an elected body is – the extent of the electorate, the degree of accountability of representatives to electors, and the degree of equality in the vote. But, of course, the entire discussion in this chapter has been founded on the assumption, usually made by public choice theorists, that voting (whether in elections or in other contexts) is a way of enabling people to get what they want. However, as we pointed out earlier, certainly in relation to electing representatives, voting can be used for purposes other than the translation of wants into collective choices. Indeed, in Britain the development of government founded on the election of representatives owed hardly anything to the idea that the purpose of elections was to construct some kind of huge matrix of wants within the state. Our next project must be to investigate how electoral systems have actually developed in Britain, and how these practices correspond to the conditions, identified in this chapter, which democratic electoral laws must meet. Natually, this requires that we pay close attention to the details of the evolution of British electoral rules.

3 The evolution of the Parliamentary electoral system

Even to the casual observer, the two most obvious features of the electoral system used for the British Parliament today are that it utilizes plurality voting and that it is based entirely on territorially-defined constituencies. Unlike most other countries in Western Europe, Britain does not employ proportional representation, nor any form of party list system. Indeed, although there were many reforms of the British electoral system in the nineteenth century and in the first half of the twentieth century, these key features of British elections have survived since medieval times. Nevertheless, as we shall see, in other respects there have been extraordinary transformations during the last two centuries in the British electoral system.

It is worth pointing out just how closely the plurality system of voting is associated with the British tradition, while it is scarcely used at all in Parliamentary elections elsewhere. Of twenty-five liberal democracies identified by Urwin, only four use the plurality system – Britain and three of its ex-colonies, Canada, New Zealand and the United States (Urwin 1987b: 6). (Of the remaining three ex-British colonies he discusses, two (Ireland and Malta) now use the single transferable vote (STV) system of proportional representation and Australia uses the alternative vote.) The British commitment to plurality voting was also revealed in the first direct elections to the European Parliament in 1979; Britain was the only country to use plurality voting for these elections, and it continues to do so, though not in Northern Ireland.

In this chapter our main focus is the historical development of the electoral system in Britain. We begin (in the first section) by examining the persistence of territorially based electoral representation in Britain, and some of the problems it has posed in modern times, because of the widespread demand that representation be democratic. Then, in the following three sections we examine other aspects of the development of British electoral rules in relation to the three elements of democratic representation which we identified in Chapter 2: the extent of the electorate (when compared with those whose interests are affected directly by the British state); the degree of accountability of representatives to their electors; and the degree of equality in the vote. Having done this, we analyse (in the subsequent section) British electoral practice in a rather different way. Political scientists have argued that any electoral system may be thought of as being composed of three different components (or 'phases') – ballot structure, constituency structure and the formula used for translating votes into seats. We modify this classification in illuminating key features of British electoral rules.

THE DEVELOPMENT OF TERRITORIAL REPRESENTATION IN BRITAIN

Representation of communities: early developments

Originally, the English Parliament was really an extension of the monarch's Council, the Privy Council (Keir 1966: 39). In the medieval period the Commons, as one of the estates of the realm, was summoned to give advice, to legislate and to raise taxes for the monarch. The basis upon which this estate was summoned was territorial, and a clear distinction was drawn between the two kinds of territorial unit which were represented in the Commons – the counties and the boroughs. (Later – in the nineteenth century – this distinction was to be a central element in controversies about Parliamentary representation, and the theoretical distinction between the two kinds of seats remained even after the 1884–5 reforms.) Before 1430 it is likely that all free householders in a county had the right to vote in an election for members of the Commons – each county having two members. While, of course, many inhabitants of counties then were not free, the franchise certainly extended beyond that of a small group. In 1430, though, the franchise was restricted by statute to freeholders whose property was worth at least 40 shillings a year – the justification for this limitation being that many people of 'low estate' had participated in elections, and that this had caused confusion (Seymour 1915: 11). But the principle, that those who had a stake in the land should be entitled to vote, remained – in effect, all that changed after 1430 was what was to count as 'having a stake'.

As centres of commerce, medieval towns sought the privileges that incorporation as boroughs would bring them – most especially being free from feudal ties to local landowners. Borough status also brought representation in the Commons – like the counties, each borough had two members. But often this representation was not regarded as much of an advantage, since it was expensive paying for members to travel to (and stay in) London for the duration of a Parliament. It was not until the sixteenth century that membership of the Commons became highly prized and contests for this privilege became widespread. Unlike the counties, boroughs themselves decided the basis of the suffrage, and this meant that there was (and continued to be until the Reform Act of 1832) enormous variation from one borough to another in the extent of the franchise. In some boroughs all householders could vote, while, at the other extreme, the vote might be restricted to the socio-economic elite, by confining the franchise to the town's 'freemen' – positions of prestige which were under the control of the borough corporation. By the eighteenth century many boroughs, either where the franchise had always been restricted or where the town's economy had undergone a major decline, were in the hands of the wealthy. Some 'rotten boroughs', such as Old Sarum, were a recognized form of property and were bought and sold quite openly.

For our purposes, one of the most interesting features of the representation of counties and boroughs in the medieval Parliament is that important socio-economic interests were being represented on a territorial basis. Nor was there any other way to do this. Land was the key resource for the medieval state, and what was more natural than to have those with a stake in it being represented through the long-standing English unit of territorial division, the county. Commerce too had to be conducted in *a place* – as, indeed, it largely has been until the 'computer revolution' of the 1970s – so that representing commercial interests by representing each borough was as self-evident as county representation. Moreover, there was an equally apparent solution to the question of how to count the votes – the candidate with the largest number of votes would be declared the winner. Medieval Europe did not know, for example, of the younger Pliny's arguments, outlined many centuries earlier, about some of the problems of voting procedures; indeed, it was not until the second half of the eighteenth century that the Frenchmen Condorcet and Borda were to make important discoveries about some of the consequences of different kinds of voting procedures.[1] The persistence of both territorial representation and plurality voting in British Parliamentary elections stems mainly from the absence of regime breakdown or crisis in the nineteenth century. Electoral reform and the extension of the franchise in that century meant that the older system of elite representation was transformed slowly into liberal democracy. As we shall see shortly, however, there are difficulties in making territorial representation compatible with democracy.

As the English Crown took over, or became merged with, other major political units in the British Isles, English Parliamentary representation was extended on a similar basis to these countries. Incorporation into the state meant granting privileges to the estates similar to those available to their English counterparts. Thus counties and boroughs in Wales, Scotland and Ireland acquired Parliamentary representation after 1536, 1707 and 1801 respectively. (However, a more restricted representation was granted to the aristocracy. Only some Scottish and Irish peers were permitted to sit in the House of Lords, so these peers were required to elect some of their fellows to represent them.)

Representation of communities: later developments

The principle of granting representation to newly acquired territories was not extended to other possessions in the British Isles (the Isle of Man and the Channel Islands), nor, more significantly, was it ever extended to colonies overseas. In spite of the successful revolt of the American colonies in 1776 on the issue of 'no taxation without representation', the British approach has remained that of not granting representation to overseas possessions. In this regard, British practice differs markedly from modern French practice; not only do French overseas possessions (such as Martinique) elect representatives to Parliament, their residents have similar voting rights in presidential elections. (The American practice is different again. Citizens of its overseas possessions (such as Guam and Puerto Rico) cannot vote in congressional or presidential elections. But both major parties allow them to select delegates to the national party conventions, at which the parties' presidential candidates are chosen.)

Only in one respect has representation in the House of Commons ever departed from a purely territorial basis – that is, from the representation of communities or, in the case of some 'rotten boroughs', supposed communities. This exception involved the university seats. From 1603 Oxford and Cambridge Universities were allowed to elect two members each. This privilege was extended to Trinity College, Dublin after 1801, to the Scottish universities in 1868, and further universities were granted the privilege in 1918, so that from then until their abolition in 1948 there was a total of twelve university seats in each Parliament.[2] If, of the seventeenth century, it could be argued that the colleges in Oxford and Cambridge did constitute communities not unlike those of a borough, this argument no longer applied in 1918. The electorates for the university seats were its graduates, many of whom by the twentieth century had little connection with their alma mater. Moreover, the principle of community representation was abandoned completely by granting seats to combined Scottish universities and, again in 1918, with the creation of two combined English university seats; these universities were separate institutions with no territorial links to each other.

One consequence of the assimilation of Wales, Scotland and Ireland was that the size of the House of Commons increased.[3] It was growing in size, in any case, from the medieval period until the eighteenth century, as new boroughs became incorporated and entitled to return MPs. In the early Tudor years there were probably rather less than 300 members, while there were 658 members following the union with Ireland in 1801. This growth in the membership of the Commons meant that it was close to reaching the maximum feasible size of a legislative chamber. This, together with the fact that by the eighteenth century many boroughs were either controlled by powerful landowners or had tiny electorates, meant that much debate about Parliamentary reform in the nineteenth century was focused on redistributing seats from some of the boroughs to the centres of population growth. Merely adding new representatives, as had been done in earlier centuries, was not a viable policy. As important as quasi-democratic arguments about fair representation in the stripping of some boroughs' seats was the fact that the very size of Parliament by the nineteenth century meant that new territorial interests could not be represented simply through the creation of new seats.

Each of the three great franchise extensions of the nineteenth century (in 1832, 1867 and 1884) was accompanied by a redistribution of Parliamentary seats. In part this was because, among some reformers at least, a desire for a wider franchise went hand-in-hand with a determination to reduce the political power of the wealthy in the smaller boroughs. But party politics also linked the two issues together; redistribution could be instituted in such a way as to reduce the impact of bringing poorer people into the electorate, so that both Tories and Whigs (and later Liberals) had a major interest in securing favourable redistributions for themselves. In 1867, for example, Disraeli gained his party's acceptance of an expanded franchise by his promise to work out the issue of county and borough boundaries to the advantage of the Conservatives. Certainly by the 1880s, when the idea of further widening the franchise in the future was more widely accepted, it could be argued that redistribution was the more important issue. As Seymour (1915: 490) noted:

in 1884, when the future of the suffrage was practically settled, not a few could be found to agree with Dilke that the redistribution of electoral power as greatly transcended the mere extension of the franchise in importance, as it did in difficulty of treatment.

If the idea that there should not be large disparities in the size of constituencies became more widespread in the nineteenth century, it was not until the massive extension of the franchise in 1918 that 'apart from the City of London and the university seats, the principle of equality in numbers between constituencies was, for the first time, fully accepted' (Butler 1963: 10). Even then the logic of this principle, that there should be periodic redistributions of seats to take account of demographic changes, was not acknowledged completely. No redistribution of seats occurred in the inter-war years, and it was not until 1944 that a procedure for effecting this regularly, in the form of a permanent Boundary Commission, was established. Moreover, as shall see in Chapter 6, there can still be considerable differences in the size of Parliamentary constituencies, especially in the years immediately preceding the adoption of new constituency boundaries.

The representation of persons

In the twentieth century one of the two conflicting principles which had been at the centre of much political debate in the nineteenth century had largely triumphed over the other. The successful principle was one associated with democracy – that it was *persons* who were to be represented in Parliament and that each person's vote was to count the same. It replaced the much older principle, that it was *communities* which were represented. Clearly, in a direct democracy there can be no conflict between principles governing representation. If representative government is to be a surrogate for direct democracy then the principle of political equality is most appropriately interpreted to require the representation of invididuals who have an equal vote.

The evolutionary transformation to democracy in Britain posed a problem for democrats, because the principle of democratic representation had to be grafted on to older practices. The problem was that of ensuring that in territorially-defined units the net result of the various elections conformed to the result that would be revealed if, say, there were a national list of candidates. In part, it is an example of the 'tyranny of small decision-making', which we discussed in Chapter 2, in that each person may not be able to choose the alternative that they would most want. However, there is also a 'technical' problem of ensuring that one vote does not count for more than another, because the size of the constituencies is different. But this kind of 'vote equality' may also conflict with a third consideration – that an election result overall conforms to the sum of individual results. In the case of competition between parties, this would require, at a minimum, that the party with the largest number of votes overall should also win the largest number of seats. But, given that people may not be distributed geographically in a way that makes it easy to create electoral districts, there is always the danger that constituencies cannot easily be created to produce this result; and, if it can be done, it may be at the price of equally sized constituencies.

As we shall see in Chapter 4, 'representation' can be understood in a number of different ways which reflect the evolution of representative practices just described. Since a constituency is both a territorial unit and a unit of population, representative practices may be defended with respect to both territory and persons. Interestingly, legislation governing contemporary electoral practice is embodied in Representation of the People Acts. 'The People' could refer to the national community or the persons within it. In Britain the triumph of the democratic principle, conceived as the representation of persons, has been far from complete. On the one hand, although it is required to make constituencies of similar size, the Boundary Commission is not allowed to create constituencies that cross county boundaries or the boundaries of London boroughs. Indeed, in a case brought by the Labour party in 1983 against the decisions of the Boundary Commission, the court ruled that Parliamentary representation did involve the representation of places. There is no requirement that constituencies be mathematically equal in size, if this would mean ignoring natural geographical boundaries. On the other hand, the Commission is not required to take account of the overall balance between the parties. Because it does not even attempt to consider the country as a whole, but looks at redistribution at the local level only, it is quite possible that a large gap could develop between total votes and seats won. Indeed, in the thirteen elections since 1945, two (1951 and February 1974) have resulted in the party with the largest number of votes securing fewer seats than the party with the second highest total. This recognition that the 'democratic revolution' has been only partly completed leads us into a discussion of the three dimensions of democracy we introduced in the last chapter.

THE EXTENT OF THE ELECTORATE

When considering the size of the British electorate in relation to the potential electorate, that is those whose interests are directly affected by the policies of the British state and who thereby have a claim to be voters, there are three elements to be examined. The first is who is legally entitled to vote in British elections; the second is the barriers or disincentives to exercising this right; and the third is the proportion of electors who, even if they can vote, cannot do so freely. We examine these three elements in turn.

Entitlement to vote

As we have seen, enfranchisement in the medieval period was dependent on having a 'stake' in the territory in which you resided. While, after 1430, the state itself determined what constituted the necessary 'stake' in the counties, in the boroughs it was left to the corporations to decide this. The Reform Act of 1832 gave the franchise to new categories of person in the counties, of whom the most numerous were tenants-at-will. For the boroughs, the Act regulated the electorate for the first time; inevitably, in some boroughs, where there had been a wider franchise beforehand, poorer people were disenfranchised by the 1831 Act and the size of the electorates there shrank. The key provision of the Act was that making freehold occupiers of houses worth at least £10 a year eligible to vote. This enfranchised a large section of the middle class, but kept out the working class. As a result about 18 per cent of adult males were entitled to vote by 1833. Overall, this upper class and middle class electorate was probably larger than the pre-1832 electorate, although how much larger has been the subject of some dispute because of disagreements about the size of the unreformed electorate. Traditionally, it has been argued that county and borough electorates each grew about 50 per cent because of the Reform Act; but other estimates suggest that the earlier electorate may have been rather smaller than was thought, so that the number of voters may have increased by as much as 80 per cent in 1832–3.

The further reforms of 1867, 1884 and 1918 progressively reduced the economic barriers to voting for men. By 1868 about 38 per cent of males were entitled to vote, by 1885 about 58 per cent were enfranchised, and the 1918 Act gave the vote to virtually all males. (A few notable exceptions, such as peers, the insane and criminals, remained and, for five years, the 1918 Act also disenfranchised conscientious objectors.) But its size, compared with previous electorates, was not the only significant feature of the post-1918 electorate. The reforms of the nineteenth century had increasingly complicated the entitlement to vote, creating new categories of entitlement, so that after 1885 'such was the "intricacy" that there was doubt as to the exact number of franchises in operation[4].' After 1918 there was only one main franchise, though with certain categories of person excluded, and two subsidiary ones – the 'business' and 'university' franchises.

It is probable that a few women did vote before 1832, but the Reform Act that year created an all-male electorate. Women were not enfranchised until 1918, and even then women under thirty remained without the vote – an anomaly that was not corrected until 1928. Moreover, as we have seen, the British practice was not to enfranchise inhabitants of its overseas colonies. But, after Irish independence in 1920, very different treatment was accorded to Northern Ireland, on the one hand, and the overseas possessions, on the other. In the case of the former, control over the province's internal affairs was devolved to a separate legislature at Stormont – this was similar to 'local control' that was to be granted to many colonies. However, Northern Irish representation at Westminster was retained, although the province did have fewer seats during the Stormont era than a similarly populated area in England would have been allocated.

Nevertheless, there is one respect in which the British electoral system does conform somewhat more than some other systems to the democratic requirement that all those whose interests are directly affected be entitled to participate in the election of representatives. Unlike, for example, the United States, the right to vote is not based entirely on citizenship. Although foreign nationals have never been permitted to vote, citizens of British colonies and Commonwealth countries have been entitled to do so, providing they are resident in Britain. Furthermore, this right has continued to be accorded to citizens of the Irish Republic. For the democrat, this arrangement is preferable to one linking voting rights strictly to citizenship, because it recognizes that those who are not citizens, but are residents of a country, are as affected as much as its citizens by public policies. Nevertheless, the UK's arrangements indicate only a very limited realization of that democratic principle.

Barriers to voting

Even when the potential electorate comprises most adults, the actual electorate may be reduced considerably by a variety of devices and procedures, which either prevent people from qualifying to vote at a particular election, or, if they are so qualified, discourage them from voting. Literacy tests are one device for disqualifying voters, while requiring proof of payment of certain taxes is a way of discouraging voters. Both of these devices have been used in the United States, which has some of the greatest institutional barriers to electoral participation and, correspondingly, by some margin, the lowest electoral turnout among the western democracies. (Even in presidential elections, turnout in the United States is not much above 50 per cent, while turnout in the UK is closer to 70 per cent of the eligible electorate, and in some other European countries turnout is as high as 80 per cent or more.)

Voter registration in Britain is comparatively easy today so that the disincentive to vote is relatively low. Since 1918 each major unit of local government has been required to have a Registration Officer who is charged with conducting a canvass of all households to establish a list of eligible voters. The householder merely has to fill in a form to be on the electoral register, and follow-up calls are made by officials on households which do not register. The costs associated with registration are borne almost entirely by the state. In contrast, the American practice since the 1890s has been to place the onus for registering on the citizen; he or she must go to the appropriate place to register. Since the chances that a single vote will determine the outcome of an election are tiny, even the costs associated with having to walk a few streets to register can lead to a major reduction in the electorate. Some scholars have seen the manipulation of electoral laws, and most especially the introduction of personal registration laws by politicians in the late 1890s, as the main reason for the dramatic decline in voter participation in US elections from that decade until the 1930s.[5] A smaller electorate would be more controllable by the dominant party, so that registration laws could be used to consolidate its position.

In Britain the electorate has not been manipulated in this way since 1918, and the barriers to voting are generally insignificant and uncontroversial. But this was not true of the period immediately preceding it. The technicalities, complications and anomalies connected with voter eligibility introduced in 1884–5 were a direct result of efforts by Whigs to manipulate the size of the electorate, and to dilute the democratic objectives of their Liberal allies (Blewett 1965: 29). Large numbers of (mainly) poorer voters, such as lodgers who moved to new lodgings, could be disenfranchised. Along with the long residence requirements in force before 1918, these sorts of restrictions probably disenfranchised about a million men from a potential electorate of less than 8,000,000. Undoubtedly, it worked to the advantage of the Conservative party.

These sorts of devices are usually associated with a pre- democratic era. It is worth remembering, though, that there is a 'cost' involved in registering to vote in Britain – namely liability to jury service. This may well be why householders have an obligation to register those eligible to vote. Many critics of the poll tax (the Community Charge) argued that one consequence of its maintenance would be to reduce the registration of voters, and that in turn this would disproportionately benefit the Conservatives because their potential voters would be the least likely to 'disenfranchise' themselves. The argument is that a significant number of poor people, who did not have to pay local rates but who would have to pay the poll tax, would seek to evade paying it by not registering themselves as liable to pay. Although the poll tax register was supposed to be administered entirely separately from the electoral register, it seems implausible that poll tax officials would not check the electoral register for possible tax-evaders, and that most of the latter, therefore, would guard against this by keeping themselves off the electoral register. Obviously, it is difficult to assess how much the registered electorate might have shrunk, because new tax arrangements have now been proposed.

Other ways of reducing the size of the electorate involve having relatively long residential qualifications or not updating regularly the list of registered voters. Both of these devices make it less likely that itinerant workers, and other members of the 'mobile poor', will be enfranchised. Once again, residence qualifications (of up to a year) were employed in many US states to reduce the size of electorates, but after a Supreme Court decision in 1972 most US states have either eliminated residential requirements altogether or have reduced them to thirty days. Before 1918 one year's residence was required in Britain too for a person to be enfranchised, and the way this was administered meant that, in practice, it took eighteen months to get on to the voting list. In 1918 the residence requirement was reduced to six months and it was abolished altogether in 1948. Although new registers of voters in Britain are compiled annually, the fact that those who move to new constituencies cannot simply add themselves to the register, but must wait for the compilation of a new one, does reduce the electorate during a year. Elections contested under 'old registers' may have significantly fewer voters than they could have – especially in areas undergoing rapid economic change.

A further factor affecting the size of the electorate at a particular election is the ease with which a person can vote. Undoubtedly, if people could merely 'tap in a vote' through a computer terminal in their home (a procedure which is not far from being technically feasible now), electoral turnout could be extremely high. The very fact that people have to go out to vote helps to reduce turnout considerably. How far they have to go, and how long they can expect to wait to vote, also influences the size of the actual electorate. In some American cities voters may have to queue for over an hour to vote, so inevitably turnout is lower than it would otherwise be. In Britain sufficient polling stations and officials are provided for this not to be a problem. One reform which has contributed to an increase in the size of the electorate is the postal vote, first introduced in 1948 for various categories of 'absentee' voters. It increases electoral turnout by about 2 per cent, and works to the advantage of the Conservatives, because middle class voters are more likely to be absent for some of the reasons which qualify a person for a postal vote. The time at which a person can vote can also serve as a barrier to voting. In the mid nineteenth century polls closed at 4.00 p.m., a device which reduced working class voting because voting hours then fell wholly within the working day. The extension of voting hours, so that today polling stations close at 10.00 p.m. (for general and European elections), means that the vast majority of eligible voters do have an opportunity to vote.

A final possible disincentive to vote is the knowledge that the result has already been decided. In the United States, for example, the declaration of results in precincts in East Coast states can occur before polling has finished in western states. In the case of a landslide election, this can diminish turnout in the final hours of polling in the west. In Britain, though, no counting of votes begins before all polls are closed, and, for example, projections of the result based on surveys of those voting earlier in the day are not released by the media until the polls close.

Freedom in voting

One of the great problems with British elections before the latter part of the nineteenth century was the control exercised over sections of the electorate – either because of clientelistic ties to patrons or because of intimidation. (Indeed, in eighteenth-century Scotland it was possible for patrons to create votes, by disposing of voting rights to their retainers, without at the same time alienating the land to which these rights were traditionally attached.) Patron–client relations cannot be eliminated by reforming the electoral laws, for the dependence of the client may be sufficiently accepted by him that he continues to vote for his patron's candidate, however much that candidate may hold views that are anathema to the client. Nevertheless, there are three aspects of electoral law reform which can help to reduce patron control – a secret ballot, an extensive franchise and effective enforcement of laws prohibiting campaign corruption and intimidation. The introduction of all three reforms in the latter part of the nineteenth century eliminated most aspects of electoral malpractice which had restricted the freedom of many voters in earlier centuries.

The secret ballot was introduced in 1872. (It had first been adopted in two Australian states in 1856, and even today it is known as the 'Australian ballot' in the United States.) But if secrecy prevented patrons, or those who had bought votes, from knowing whether their clients had carried out their part of the mutual arrangement, its effects would still be limited if the electorate remained small. When they constituted the greater part of the electorate, large numbers of 'clients' could not all rebel against their masters and collectively get away with it. Thus franchise extension and the elimination of tiny borough constituencies were also an important element in freeing voters from unwanted influence. Finally, the passage of the Corrupt and Illegal Practices Act in 1883, and more especially its rigorous implementation, transformed British electoral practice. Bribery had long been a feature of elections – before the sixteenth century, however, 'not to get into Parliament but to keep out of it' (O'Leary 1962: 2). Intimidation too was long established, as was fraud. But, while in the United States many of the electoral practices associated with nineteenth-century 'boss politics' survived (the Chicago machine added crucial votes to John Kennedy's total in Illinois in 1960), twentieth-century British elections have been remarkable for the absence of overtly venal practices.

THE ACCOUNTABILITY OF ELECTED TO ELECTORS

The idea of accountability by representatives to those they represent is multi-faceted, and in the space available here only a few aspects of the accountability provided by British elections can be examined. In this section we examine four of the most important aspects of the accountability of MPs to the electorate: how frequently they must be subjected to re-election, the effectiveness of the electoral system in removing unpopular representatives, the role of parties in structuring voter choice to effect accountability, and the ease with which voters can identify and help to elect particular candidates.

Constraints of the need to be re-elected

Models of representative democracy based on assumptions of rational choice by the participants have long demonstrated the constraints that

the need to seek re-election can have on the behaviour of representatives. When an elected representative is prohibited from seeking
re-election (as is the President of Mexico and the Governor of
Kentucky), or has decided to retire from office, the need to be bound by
the views of his or her electorate are much reduced. (For studies of the
effects on the behaviour of elected officials in American local
government, see Prewitt and Nowlin (1969) and Prewitt (1970).)
Elections can make representatives directly accountable, then, only
when they can and will seek re-election. The electoral system in Britain,
of course, does not limit MPs with respect to the number of terms they
may serve.

Equally important in generating accountability is the length of time
between each election. An overly long interval will increase the
opportunity of representatives to enact policies that are not wanted by
the voters; this is partly because unpopular measures from earlier years
may be forgotten, and partly because it increases the number of 'items'
in the 'package' of policies which form a government's record, and the
larger the package the less likely a government will be 'punished' for
highly unpopular individual policies. (This problem for voters, that they
cannot choose policies individually, but only an entire 'package'
presented to them, is known by public choice theorists as 'full-line
supply'.) From 1715 to 1911 the British Parliament could have a 'life' of
up to seven years, but this was then reduced to five years. In fact, few
peace-time Parliaments have lasted this long – the average length being
three and a half years in the period 1945 87, which is much in line with
legislative terms in other liberal democracies. However, although many
nineteenth-century democrats advocated annual Parliaments, accountability to voters is also reduced if the interval between elections is too
brief. Representatives then have little incentive to promote policies
which would produce benefits in the long term but which may impose
costs in the short term; they would always be penalized by an electorate
that is more aware of the costs. The policy process would be geared too
much towards improving the short-term popularity of representatives.
Indeed, this is a problem evident in the US House of Representatives
which is subject to re-election every two years. Major policy initiatives
are much more difficult to effect in the second year of the term than they
are in the first, because of the imminence of the next election. Today
hardly any democratic reformers in Britain advocate legislative terms as
short as this.

Of far greater concern now is the advantage a governing party enjoys
in timing its policies so as to have the most favourable impact in the
run-up to the next election. Studies have demonstrated that various

macro-economic variables are closely correlated with the timing of elections (for example, Tufte 1978). Some commentators in Britain have seen the ability of British governments to manipulate the economy in this way as the product of the government's power to determine (in most circumstances) the date of a general election. This is a mistake. Economic manipulation also occurs in political systems where the timing of an election is fixed by law. The relevant difference between government-determined and fixed-term elections is that under the former system a government can call an early election in circumstances which are favourable to it. It is the knowledge of when an election will occur that gives a government its principal advantage, and which weakens the system of accountability through elections, fixed-term or otherwise.

The only way to reform the electoral system radically in this respect would be to deny all representatives of as much knowledge as possible of the likely date of the next election. One way of doing this would be to hold a weighted lottery every day, once a Parliament was, say, three years old, up to the last-but-one day of the life of the Parliament. When the lottery deemed there would be an election, Parliament would be dissolved immediately and the election campaign begin. Leaving aside possible problems of the disruption to Parliamentary business in the middle of a session, there is still one serious disadvantage to such a scheme. In Parliamentary systems, though not under the separation of powers as practised in the United States, governments may always engineer Parliamentary defeats to secure an election at a favourable time, and it is not clear that this device would not be used to allow governments to retain the advantage they presently enjoy. Even in West Germany, where governments cannot 'call' an election as they can in Britain, a Parliamentary defeat was engineered after the fall of the SPD-led coalition government in 1982 to allow the new coalition to have the election it wanted. While such practices might not negate completely the effects of the lottery scheme, it is clear that the problem of making governments electorally accountable is a complex one.

Effectiveness of elections in removing unpopular representatives

One of the principal qualities that a democrat would want of an electoral system is that it does not pose peculiar difficulties for the electorate in removing unpopular representatives – or, at the level of the state, an unpopular government. We have just noted one such obstacle in modern western democracies – the ability of a governing party to manipulate an economy to its own electoral advantage. Further obstacles are posed by the kind of electoral formula used in Britain – namely, plurality voting. With a minor exception, this method of aggregating votes is the only one to have been used in British Parliamentary elections: proportional representation was employed in some of the university seats after 1918. (The British Parliament, however, has imposed proportional representation on other bodies for which it was deemed appropriate – most notably for the Stormont Parliament in the 1920s, for the Northern Ireland Convention set up in the 1970s, and now for local and European elections in that province.) There are two problems posed by plurality voting which must be raised here in a discussion of accountability.

One limitation of the British system is that those opposed to a particular candidate or a governing party may vote only for one of the other parties' candidates. The voter's choice is limited by what alternatives happen to be available at that particular election. There is no provision for either 'writing in' the name of someone not on the ballot (a device employed in some American states), nor is there a box provided at the bottom of the ballot so that the voter may opt for 'none of the above'. Some American writers have argued in favour of such a device, because it would enable the voter to protest against the structuring of electoral choice for him or her. Of course, such a mechanism would require some second election (or other means of choosing a representative) should 'none of the above' attain a plurality. Even if it did nothing else, this procedure might provide a better indication than at present of the degree of voter alienation from existing parties.

More generally, though, plurality voting suffers from the disadvantage that it may fail to produce the unseating of candidates or parties opposed by a majority (possibly an intense majority) of voters. If the opposition vote is split between two or more opponents none of them may be able to defeat a candidate who has only minority support. To explain this point further, it is useful here to introduce the concept of a 'Condorcet winner'. If there are three candidates, A, B, and C, and A would beat B in an election involving just the two of them, and A would also beat C in a similar one-on-one contest, then A meets the condition of being a 'Condorcet winner'. It seems evidently desirable that the electoral system should select a Condorcet winner, if there is one. But as McLean (1987: 156) has said of plurality voting: 'It often fails to select a Condorcet winner, and may sometimes select a Condorcet loser, or "dominated" outcome: that is, an outcome which loses the pairwise vote with every other.' In an election where there are only two candidates, or two parties, the problem of the election winner not being a 'Condorcet winner' does not arise, of course. But, apart from the period 1931–59 when it appeared that a complete two-party system might be emerging, British politics since 1918 has typically involved candidates of three or more parties contesting a seat, with the third party securing a sufficient share of the vote to raise doubts as to whether the winner would be a 'Condorcet winner'. Furthermore, in the early to mid 1980s, it appeared that genuinely three-party politics was about to emerge, and that in many Parliamentary seats 'Condorcet losers' would be elected. In such circumstances the strong possibility exists that a highly unpopular government might be sustained in power by the inability of electors to demonstrate their opposition to it effectively.

Parties and the structuring of the vote

Political parties simplify choice for the voter in two related respects. First, they make it easier for voters to know the kind of policies a particular candidate might support; when there are large numbers of candidates seeking publicity in a country, it may be difficult for voters to 'hear' anything amidst the 'white noise' of electoral competition. Second, in a territorially based electoral system, parties enable the voters to see some connection (in terms of likely public policies) between the choices they make and the choices made by others elsewhere. In fact, the British party system provides for greater accountability of this kind than does, for example, the American party system, with its loosely structured, unprogrammatic parties. The point to be emphasized here is that the degree of accountability to voters that an electoral system can provide must depend on factors outside the formal electoral rules. These rules influence the degree of accountability, but there is no set of rules which can wholly compensate for factors in the socio-political sphere which restrict the ability of parties to act as 'teams' and to simplify choices for voters.

There are many factors which contribute to the cohesion of political parties, but we cannot digress to discuss this matter here. It is worth noting, however, that there was one major transformation in the British electoral system in the nineteenth century that might, conceivably, have made it less easy for cohesive parties to organize. As it was, it had little effect on the development of party organization. This was the switch to the use of single-member districts. The traditional English practice was for both counties and boroughs to have two members each – chosen in a single election. (In 1790 there were only five single-member seats in England, the remaining sixty-nine single-member seats in the Commons all being in Scotland and Wales. In fact, there were no double-member seats at all in these two countries.) The redistribution of seats resulting from Parliamentary reform increased the use of the single-member constituencies in both counties and boroughs. With the exception of the brief period from 1868 to 1884 when some three-member constituencies were created, the nineteenth century witnessed the transformation to a single-member system; after 1885 double-member constituencies were rare, although these seats did not disappear completely until 1950. In theory, multi-member districts make it easier for centralized party organizations to establish control at the expense of local elites – for the good reason that they require more election resources, which more centralized parties are better placed to supply. Certainly in America, the demise of multi-member districts in many state legislatures in the last thirty to forty years has helped to weaken party organizations there (Ware 1985: 119–24). Of course, various other conditions were much more favourable to strong parties in Britain, so that the virtual elimination of the double-member constituencies after 1885 had limited adverse effects on the development of more centralized parties.

The ease of identifying and helping to elect candidates

One of the features of Parliamentary elections which is sometimes overlooked is that there is actually a list of candidates; that there is such a list makes the task of voters who wish to use their vote effectively much easier. Not all elections require, or even allow, candidates to declare themselves formally, and in such elections it is more difficult for voters to use their vote strategically. Many democrats prefer voting systems which encourage sincere voting, but, when sincere voting is necessitated by a lack of knowledge of the possible behaviour of others, it can also facilitate the persistence of control by dominant minorities. For example, when magistrates elect the chairman and deputy-chairmen of their bench, they merely write down their own preferences on a piece of paper: any serving magistrate may be voted for, so that it is difficult for groups of magistrates to coordinate their activities to ensure that their most preferred peers are elected. This lack of 'fine tuning' in their electoral process makes it more likely that the better-known (and usually senior) magistrates will be the ones chosen. In Parliamentary elections, though, candidacies must be declared formally and a financial deposit paid, which is non-returnable if the candidate fails to secure a minimum proportion of the vote. (Today the deposit is £500 and the minimum share of the vote which must be obtained is 5 per cent.)

Voting procedures vary enormously in the extent to which they make it easy for a person to vote for the candidates he or she actually prefers. Generally, British procedures have been remarkably simple and have facilitated this choice. Two minor exceptions to this, which are no longer evident, should be noted. In the three-member constituencies of the period 1868–84, each voter could cast only two votes. The uninformed voter who wished to help elect an entire party slate would have had difficulty knowing how to use this vote most effectively. (In fact, it was the success of the Liberal caucus in Birmingham, in organizing electorates effectively to overcome this problem, that was to contribute to the transformation of British party organization in the last quarter of the century.) Another, but longer surviving, anomaly in the British Parliamentary electoral system, which made it more difficult for voters to identify candidates, was that in elections before 1970 candidates could not identify their parties on the ballot form. Since, for more than a century, British elections had been primarily directed towards electing parties rather than individuals to Parliament, the effect of this was to increase marginally the random element in voter selection, because some voters would be confused in the voting booth as for whom they really wanted to vote. But British voters have not been subjected to the confusion generated by the 'long ballot', evident in some American states, where the sheer number of offices which must be selected at one time creates what is known as 'voter fatigue' – a failure to vote at all for many of the lesser offices.

EQUALITY OF THE VOTE

One issue of vote equality we may leave aside (until Chapter 7) is whether plurality voting necessarily provides for an unequal treatment of some voters. These are voters whose first preference is for a candidate who finishes third (or lower) in an election won with less than 50 per cent of the vote. There remain, though, two issues of vote equality in the British electoral system to be addressed here. The first is that of the inequality in the size of electorates in constituencies. Obviously, there has been a marked reduction in this inequality since the nineteenth century. Today, the largest constituency is never more than about twice the size of the smallest one, at least immediately after a reapportionment, while after 1832 the largest was sixty times bigger than the smallest and after 1885 there was still a 700 per cent variation (Butler 1963: 213). However, in addition to the fact that even today the Boundary Commission is mandated to take some account of the 'representation of places', and not just people, there is a further source of inequality in constituency size. This is the problem of Scotland and Wales, which have remained 'overrepresented' in Parliament even since the setting up of the Boundary Commission. Relative population decline in these two countries would suggest that, at each redistribution of seats, either they are allocated fewer seats or the number of seats in the Commons is increased to give greater representation to England. However, the former alternative has always been held to be politically inexpedient. And, while there has been a gradual increase in the size of the Commons, complete removal of the anomaly would require a very considerable increase in seats – thereby, arguably, making the Commons much too large a legislative chamber. In any case, because of the greater strength of both the Labour party and the Liberal Democrats in Scotland and Wales, the anomaly helps to counterbalance the pro-Conservative bias in the distribution of seats in England.

The other issue is that it is only since 1948 that 'one adult person one vote' has been the operating principle in Britain. In the earlier period some people had more than one vote. Plural voting existed before 1832, but it was the complicated extensions to the franchise in 1832, 1867 and 1884 which greatly extended this system. This is somewhat ironic, since mid-century proposals to create 'fancy franchises', or double votes for certain categories of people, consistently failed to win Parliamentary approval. It has been estimated, though, that in 1911 about 7 per cent of the electorate (which was about 5–6,000,000 people) was entitled to more than one vote (Blewett 1965: 46). A small number of people may have had as many as twenty or more votes, all of which they could cast quite legally. In the nineteenth century plural voting was designed quite explicitly for partisan ends. The process had been started by the Whigs in 1832 who (in Blewett's words) 'threw' the borough freeholders into the counties, and, although by the end of the century it was the Conservatives and their Unionist allies who were the principal beneficiaries, the Conservative advantage was probably only a slight one (Blewett 1965: 48 and 50). Although even some Conservatives, including Disraeli, objected to multiple voting as unfair, the principle that a man could vote in as many different constituencies as he was registered in was adhered to until the 1918 reforms. Only one vote, however, could be cast in each constituency.

A more restricted form of plural voting was retained after 1918. The occupancy of business premises worth more than £10 annually entitled businessmen (and, from 1928 to 1944, their wives) to a vote. But, once again, voting twice in the same constituency was not permissible. The other form of plural voting was in the university seats. Since the business vote was never more than about 1.5 per cent of the total vote in the inter-war period, and the university seats constituted only about 2 per cent of the total seats in the Commons, after 1918 there was a marked decline in the potential effect of plural voting. Nevertheless, both franchises were abolished in 1948. Today no person is entitled to more than one vote.

THE ELEMENTS OF ELECTORAL SYSTEMS

In comparing electoral systems, it is useful to develop a framework within which to understand their different elements. A number of typologies of electoral systems have been constructed by political scientists, many of which concentrate on the different ways in which the votes are actually aggregated.[6] Perhaps a more useful approach, because it is broader in scope, is that of Rae who was explicitly concerned with systems involving inter-party competition, and who suggested that there were three 'phases' of an electoral system. Particular electoral systems could vary in regard to each of these phases, which were: '(1) balloting as a specification of the voter's role in deciding the election, (2) districting as a limiting factor in the translation of votes to seats, and (3) electoral formulae as key factors in the translation of votes to seats' (Rae 1971: 16). In effect these three phases are concerned with (1) how votes can be cast (or the ballot structure), (2) the constituency structure – the territorial (or other basis) on which seats are allocated – and (3) the rules used for translating votes into seats. Although Rae himself defines these phases rather narrowly, they can form the basis for a broader way of classifying electoral systems, which is applicable not just to electoral systems in which there is inter-party competition. To see how this classification works we will indicate how the different features of the British electoral system fit into it.

Ballot structure

There are several dimensions of ballot structure to which attention must be drawn. Rae himself distinguishes only two types of ballot, categorical and ordinal, but, as Blais argues, this distinction actually conceals two different dimensions. One is the number of votes each voter is allowed to cast, while the other is the type of information they may provide (Blais 1988: 104). But this first dimension may be further sub-divided: how many votes may voters cast on their ballot and how many ballots are they allowed to complete? As we have seen, since the abolition of the business and university franchises, British voters may complete only one ballot. On this ballot they may cast a vote for only one candidate; in a single-member constituency using plurality voting, this is the only way that voting can be arranged. However, in multi-member constituencies, a voting system can provide the voter either with as many votes as there are seats or with fewer votes than seats. Both systems have been used in Britain in the past. In the double-member constituencies voters had two votes, but in the brief period when there were some three-member constituencies, a voter could still cast only two votes in those constituencies.

As to the second dimension Blais mentions, the only information British voters can provide on the ballot form is who their first-choice candidate is; they cannot show who their second or third choices are, nor can they show any intensity of preference between candidates. This feature is often associated with plurality voting just as proportional representation is normally thought of as involving the opportunity for voters to provide additional information about their preferences. But this connection is not a necessary one. Not all proportional systems give the voter more than one vote – party list systems where there is no voter choice over candidates are instances of this practice. Moreover, there could be a Parliament using plurality voting in single-member constituencies in which voters could indicate their second-choice candidate; in the event of a tie in a three-candidate contest the winner would be determined by the greatest number of second-choice ballots.[7]

Blais also shows that there is another dimension of ballot structure not discussed by Rae – whom or what the voter may vote for. In Parliamentary elections, he or she could vote either for an individual candidate, or (as in some party list systems, such as Iceland) only for a party, or yet again for some combination of the two (as in Belgium). In Britain, of course, voters may vote only for an individual candidate, who is most likely the representative of a party, but they can show support for a party only indirectly, through voting for its candidate.

Yet another feature of ballot structure is whether voters can vote for whom or what they like, or merely for those alternatives (if any) presented to them on the ballot form. Unlike the British magistrate voting for a chairman, the voter in a general election does have a list of declared candidates from whom to choose. Indeed, if he or she votes and does not merely spoil the ballot form, the British voter must select a candidate only from among those appearing on the ballot. There is no provision in Britain for writing in the name of a candidate not on the ballot, nor is there a final alternative on the ballot form, 'none of the above'.

Finally, there is a crucial aspect of the voter's role in deciding an election which modern students of electoral systems often ignore, but which was at the centre of many debates about electoral reform in the nineteenth century: whether the ballot should be secret or open. While nation states today employ a secret ballot, it was not employed in any country until 1856 (in Australia). What voters can do in casting a vote in an election (for example, whether they can use it to promote their own interests, or must exercise judgement in deciding what is best for the country) is determined partly by whether that vote is open to scrutiny by their fellow citizens.

Constituency structure

There are three variables to consider under the heading of 'constituency structure', which constitutes the second 'phase' of an electoral system.

1 Is the election conducted 'at large' or is the body to which an election is to be made divided into constituencies? Unlike the French presidency, say, or a nation-wide party list system of the Icelandic kind, British Parliamentary elections are fought in separate constituencies.
2 Are these constituencies organized on a territorial basis, or on some other basis? We have seen already that British elections are organized purely on a territorial basis. But this is not the only way of providing for representation. For example, following the arguments of some of the early twentieth-century English pluralists, it might be proposed that representatives be elected to Parliament on some other basis – such as in non-territorial constituencies of trade union members or employers' organizations.
3 Are the constituencies single-member or multi-member? Again, we have seen that Britain has shifted over two centuries from using predominantly double-member constituencies to the sole use of single-member constituencies.

The electoral formula

An electoral formula is the way in which the votes are allocated to whatever it is (candidate or party) that the people have voted for – in a Parliament it is the rules governing how votes are translated into seats. There are three main kinds of formulae.

Majority

For a candidate to be elected using this formula he or she must obtain more than 50 per cent of the vote. Some majoritarian systems, such as that used in the election of the Pope or the nomination of Democratic presidential candidates earlier this century, require that the winner obtain an even larger majority than this; of course, these systems, which are better described as super-majoritarian systems, cannot guarantee that there will ever be a winner.[8] There are two kinds of simple majoritarian systems: the Alternative Ballot (used, for example, in Australian Parliamentary elections) and the Second Ballot (which is used in French presidential elections). Both provide that there is a 'final contest' between only two candidates (or parties) so that the winning candidate must have received over half the vote. These systems have never been employed in British Parliamentary elections.

Plurality

In this system the candidate or party with the largest number of votes wins, even if the proportion of the total vote taken by the winning candidate is small. In some primary elections for the US Congress winning candidates have sometimes secured less than 20 per cent of the vote, but the party system in Britain normally ensures that the winner would have received at least a third of the total vote. Only in rural Wales and Scotland, where there have been close contests involving Conservative, Labour, Liberal and Nationalist candidates, does the vote of a winning candidate today ever dip below the 30 per cent level.

Proportionality

Proportional systems attempt to provide for a 'fit' between the votes cast and the share of the seats (in a Parliament) accorded to each party. Some proportional systems provide for a greater fit between votes and seats than others, and in some cases the fit is actually worse than in some non-proportional systems. For British Parliamentary elections the STV system is the proportional system most canvassed by reformers, and it is the only form of proportional representation ever to have been used in British elections – for some of the university seats between 1918 and 1945. Indeed, it could be argued that STV is almost 'as British' as plurality voting: of the countries listed by Urwin (1987b), the only two to use STV are ex-British colonies.

It is important to recognize that these different electoral formulae rely on utilizing different information about a voter's preferences. A plurality system is concerned exclusively with a voter's first preference and not his or her lower-order preferences. In the first instance, a majority system makes use only of first-order preferences but second (and subsequently yet lower-order) preferences may have to be counted to produce a winner. Proportional systems are more varied. It is possible to devise a proportional electoral formula which relies solely on first preferences – for example, a single national party list system could take this form. However, many of the proportional systems which are actually used depend on the availability of voters' lower-order preferences – they could not produce proportionality without them. Moreover, proponents of proportionality are often attracted to electoral systems which use it because, in practice, they usually do involve weight being given to lower-order preferences when translating votes into seats. For example, while those advocating the introduction of STV in Britain primarily stress the alleged unfairness in the distribution of seats produced by the plurality system, some of them also assert that PR has the merit of allowing voters for the candidates of one party to express a preference between candidates of other parties.

CONCLUDING REMARKS

There is always a danger in believing that practices or rules that one is familiar with are somehow 'natural', and that anything that is different is merely a 'deviation'. Certainly, early British students of electoral systems tended to take this view of the British system in comparison with others. Like the two-party system, plurality voting in territorially defined constituencies was seen as the standard form and other systems were the deviants. But like the coelacanth, that curious survivor from the age of dinosaurs, the British electoral system (and its offspring in the ex-colonies) might be regarded as an oddity among the electoral systems used in modern liberal democracies. A medieval system of electing representatives has survived because of the curiously evolutionary transformation of British politics in the nineteenth century. But this image of stasis in the British electoral system can also be very misleading, because there have been some quite radical changes in that system over the last 200 years. These changes have included the introduction of the idea that people (and not just territory) should be represented; the evolution of universal suffrage at the expense of property-based franchises; the abolition of plural franchises; the elimination of two-member constituencies; and the introduction of the secret ballot. Whether this system of government by elected representatives is a particularly democratic one is an issue which we address in the next chapter.

4 Electoral systems and democracy

INTRODUCTION

This chapter discusses the claims of British electoral practice to be democratic. Chapter 2 has already introduced some of the considerations relevant to this enquiry, such as the relation between elections and six methods of arriving at a decision. Chapter 3 has traced the development of 'one person, one vote' and established that this popular interpretation of the meaning of democracy is a relatively recent practice. The present chapter has three aims. First, to draw that discussion together, and to extend it, in considering what might be required of a democractic political system. Secondly, to ask how far existing political practice in Britain has the capacity to fulfil those requirements. And thirdly, to use this identification of the connections between democracy and electoral systems to introduce the comparison between plurality voting and alternative systems which will form the subject of Chapter 7. Our focus will be on the relations between elections, representation, and democracy.

The British political system has come to embody the idea of one person one vote in its electoral practice. Since the British system is also regarded as democratic, it is tempting to conclude, as many people who need only a rough and ready account are willing to do, that democracy means one person, one vote. But this, as we have seen, is inadequate. Put bluntly, democracy does not require elections, and the mere existence of elections does not prove the existence of a democratic political system.

Again, the British polity is claimed to be a representative system (Birch 1964: 13). Let us identify the different levels at which representativeness might be of concern under the British system. First, there is the relation between the individual voter, the constituency, and the person elected. Secondly, there is the relation between the aggregate of constituency representatives and the country (in both geographical and political terms). Thirdly, there is the relation between the representative assembly and the government. Finally, there is the relation between the government and the community as a whole. We shall want to consider each of these relations below.

Obviously we must acknowledge that there are many problems associated with clarifying the meaning of democracy (for example, May 1978), and it will help to employ three distinctions in the discussion.[1] First, we may distinguish between democracy conceived as a method, and democracy conceived as an ideal. Secondly, we may distinguish between direct democracy and indirect democracy. Thirdly, we may distinguish between democracy considered in relation to a single decision, and democracy considered in relation to an ongoing political process. These distinctions are interconnected, and it is useful to explore them in turn.

Democracy as a method and as an ideal

Political scientists concerned to explain the operation of systems of government are inclined to adopt a 'positive' view of democracy merely as a method.[2] For example, Schumpeter's definition of the democratic method was:

> that institutional arrangement for arriving at political decisions in which individuals acquire the power to decide by means of a competitive struggle for the people's vote.
>
> (Schumpeter 1967: 173–4)

Our characterization of democracy, by contrast, acknowledged that it was one of a number of decision-making methods, but we built into our description of the method a number of normative considerations. Democracy is centred on the idea of political equality: as a method, this suggests equality in voting resources, and hence 'one person, one vote'; but as an ideal, it represents a goal which political systems approach to a greater or lesser degree. Clearly the ideal of political equality is not satisfied by the mere equality of votes, even though, when a decision is taken by voting, equal votes are a necessary condition of political equality.

Direct and indirect democracy.

This distinction was introduced in Chapter 1. In a direct democracy, individuals collectively choose what policy they will jointly pursue, or what law they will adopt. They may find it necessary to employ a voting system to do this; or there might be a more informal system which rests on the emergence of a consensus. For example, a group of friends deciding how to spend their time together might have the options of having a drink, going for a walk and so on. While they might end up by voting in order to decide what they should do, it is much more likely that a 'decision' would emerge from discussion and consultation. If this is truly described as a democratic decision, then it is obviously possible that democracy could exist without any voting at all, or with voting only on policies, and therefore without the use of a system of election.

Indirect democracy refers to the familiar situation in which there is more than one vote or decision separating the individual voter from the collective outcome. Usually the extra vote, the additional level of voting, exists because the voter chooses a representative who then votes on policy. Indirect democracy is typically representative democracy, and this is undoubtedly its most important form. But, as we have seen, not all elections are aimed at choosing a representative – we gave the example of the Pope. A rather different case is that of the elected dictator. In a crisis, a dictator (who was to determine policy single-handedly) might be chosen, and such a dictator need not represent anyone. More generally, an election can produce an officeholder who is allowed to determine matters authoritatively. We must separate, therefore, democrats' concern with the procedure by which an office holder is selected, from their concern with the process of subsequent decision-making.

Evaluating single decisions and evaluating processes

A single decision, considered in isolation from the entire political process of which it is part, may be evaluated by reference to criteria derived from a commitment to democracy. For example, democrats are concerned that particular policy outcomes should correspond to citizens' preferences. On the other hand, the criteria of democracy are used to assess political systems as a whole. This means that we might find instances of democratic decisions within highly undemocratic polities, and undemocratic decisions within polities which are broadly democratic. An elected dictator may well be chosen by democratic methods, but the procedures by which he or she subsequently governs are specifically intended not to be themselves democratic.

THE PLACE OF ELECTIONS IN DEMOCRACY

In the light of the distinctions we have just drawn, we can see that elections are a contingent feature of democracy. We can now develop the claim that democracy does not require elections, and that the existence of elections does not demonstrate the existence of democracy, by considering these examples.

Direct democracy, we suggested, need not use a voting system at all, much less the apparatus of elections. This is clear from the example of the friends jointly deciding how to spend their evening.

As the example of the elected dictator makes clear, it is possible that there could be the occasion for an election without the existence of 'process' democracy. However we think democracy should be characterized, two elements in most views are missing in the case of an elected dictator. First, there need be no correspondence at all between his or her decisions and what anyone else wants or prefers. Secondly, the dictator's power need have no temporal limit beyond that given by nature (although the ancient Republics aimed to give the dictator power only for a fixed term). Again, in Hobbes's political theory the sovereign is authorized to act by his or her future subjects but not required to submit to their approval again (Hobbes n.d.: Chapters 16–19). For both these reasons, there is no accountability.

There are many political systems in which elections occur but which have a doubtful democratic character. For example, there were elections in Eastern Europe even before the upheavals of 1988–9, but if there was only one candidate, or if all candidates were chosen by the Communist party, then another element commonly identified with democracy is missing – that of choice. (It is this choice that reform movements like Solidarity and New Forum aimed to achieve.) It is possible to maintain the connection between indirect democracy and elections by suggesting that these are not real elections, that election itself contains the idea of choice. This essentialist manoeuvre is unsatisfactory, however, because the major issue does not involve the question of whether there is more than one alternative on which to vote but the closeness of some one alternative to the preference of any given voter. As we have already seen, elections can be classified or graded with respect to the sort of information the voter is able to convey in using his or her vote, and the complaint about elections in one-party states is usually that the voter can convey a preference from within only a narrow range of choice.

Moreover, a choice may be made without an electoral system by means which might be defensible in terms of some elements of democracy – for example, by a lottery between candidates who will serve for a set term, whose policies equally correspond to some aggregation of citizens' preferences.

The example of elective dictatorship shows that the presence of elections does not imply that the person selected has a representative character. Elections designed to select representatives will have to fulfil particular requirements appropriate to that task. Part of this chapter will be devoted to specifying those requirements.

For all these reasons, there is only a contingent connection between democracy and electoral systems. But although this is an important point, we must be wary of pushing it too far. Because if our aim is to achieve democracy, or as much democracy as possible, and if we decide to employ an electoral system to pursue that aim (perhaps for reasons of practicality), then we shall have certain requirements which we shall want that system to meet. All that we have established so far is that one person one vote is neither necessary nor sufficient to ensure the democratic character of the polity. Nor, of course, does it provide us with much guidance on how to discriminate between types of electoral system. For example, we might want to ask whether plurality voting or proportional representation contributes more to democracy, but we shall not be able to get far with an answer if our idea of democracy is simply one person one vote. In Chapter 7, we shall be tackling that issue, but we must first take our discussion of the connections between electoral systems and democracy rather further.

If we begin from the distinction between direct and indirect democracy, we can try to identify the characteristics of democracy in the first case, and ask how far the second can reproduce them, or add additional features, or achieve the same ends by different means. This route is not available to someone who identifies democracy with the existence of an electoral system. Political scientists, like Schumpeter, concerned to produce (what they think of as) a realistic descriptive account of democracy have gone almost that far in defining democracy in terms of the existence of competitive elections (rather than mere elections, taking account of the point about choice mentioned earlier). The alternative is to think of democracy, not in terms of particular institutions, but in terms of ideals, aims or ends. On this alternative view, then, democracy might be a set of ideals which value popular rule, political equality, political participation and so on. This second view is the one adopted here. In looking at direct democracy, we are asking what the ideals, aims or ends associated with it might be, in order to compare the extent to which these could be met, or alternatives offered, in an indirect system.

DIRECT DEMOCRACY

'Looking at direct democracy', however, is not quite so straightforward until we decide whether we want to look at political theories which have advocated or defended it or whether we want to look at a particular political system which we take to embody direct democracy. Because of the history of the term, the examples of direct democracy which are often cited in these discussions come from classical polities, in virtue of the term having been applied to those systems. By present-day standards, however, those polities had features which would be regarded as non-democratic or anti-democratic. For example, they were built on slavery, the citizen body was much smaller than the population as a whole, because of the exclusion of at least both women and slaves from participation, and there were usually highly oligarchic components in the constitution (Dahl 1989: 13–23). In view of these difficulties, it is perhaps better to look at a different situation, such as that of members of a club gathered at an annual general meeting. In this sense we are looking at a simple model of direct democracy, restricted to the (relatively) small field defined by the purposes of the club. Let us suppose that it is a social club.

Four characteristics of democracy were introduced in Chapter 1. They were: that everyone should be able to make proposals to the group; that everyone can engage in discussion of issues; that there should be equality in participation; and that procedures be used which link individuals' views, opinions and preferences to policies. The example of a group of friends deciding on a joint social outing, then, may well fit these requirements, simply because of the informality and intimacy of the setting. But even here it is worth remembering that equality of participation depends on the distribution of resources, which in this informal case may well depend on the strength of personalities and so on. And most people will be familiar with the difficulties that arise, even in such simple cases, when there is no broad economic equality in the group – for an option which is easily affordable for one person (going to a night club, say) may well be an unwarranted expense for another. Furthermore, it is important to see that if we compare the extent to which the four characteristics are present in two different situations, we are likely to find that there is more of one feature and less of another: for example, more equal participation in situation A than situation B, but procedures that more closely link preferences with policies in B than in A. Both from the formulation of the four characteristics just given, and from thinking about this very simple example of the friends' choice, we can establish that democracy as it is conceived here is inevitably a matter of degree. Institutions, arrangements and practices are more or less democratic; there is no simple feature which will distinguish democracy from non-democracy[3].

The example of a social club draws upon, but develops, the situation of the friends, and identifies some further considerations relevant to direct democracy. The identification of these features will help us to see the expectations that have been held of indirect democracy, and some of its necessary limitations. At the Annual General Meeting (AGM) of the Erewhon Social Club, all members are invited to attend. The executive committee which has been running the Club for the last year comes to the end of its term of office, and a new committee is elected. The Agenda for the meeting contains proposals for policies – concerning items like which drinks should be on sale, which nights entertainment should be provided – and, quite possibly, proposals for changes in the constitution of the Club. It also has an agenda item for 'any other business' so members can begin a discussion of matters which concern them without having to have put down a formal agenda item in advance.

In this situation, the AGM provides an instance of direct democracy, even though there are elections for a committee to regulate the Club's affairs between the General Meetings. At an AGM, the members determine policy by voting on resolutions after discussion and they can alter the constitution. They can also overturn any executive decisions which have been made which are unpopular. In these ways, the members are sovereign during an AGM, even though there is an executive committee during the year. By analogy, direct democracy in a political context is sometimes identified with popular sovereignty and with the pursuit of the people's will. Rousseau famously thought of democracy in this way. He rejected the representation of sovereignty as incompatible with freedom, and mocked English pretensions about their free government. The English were free, he said, only when they voted (Rousseau 1913: 78).

When the members of the Erewhon Social Club elect a committee, they are choosing a group from amongst their own number to regulate the affairs of the Club until next year. Any member is entitled to stand for office. 'Regulation' here involves carrying out the decisions of the AGM (implementing policy) and taking decisions about new issues which arise. But the existence of the executive does not substantially diminish the sovereignty of the members in general. This is partly because policy is always subject to revision at the meetings, even if policy has been determined by the executive in response to a new issue; it is partly because annual re-election provides for close accountability, so that policy determination and implementation is quite likely to accord with the wishes of the membership (particularly if the committee members want to be re-elected); and it is partly because such clubs almost always provide for Emergency General Meetings (EGMs) to be called, either by the executive or on production of the signatures of a set number of members, which will enable the executive to refer difficult new problems to the whole Club, or dissatisfied members to challenge the committee about its activites. Another important consideration is that the executive members are likely to be those who use the Club's facilities quite extensively; peripherally involved members of clubs rarely stand for office. This means both that the executive members have an interest in the flourishing of the organization, and that they are available to consult members and to be lobbied by them. In this case, then, indirect democracy and direct democracy co-exist. The former is a pragmatic response to the costs of permanent direct democracy, but it does not seriously diminish it.

We have argued that representative democracy is only one form of indirect democracy. Persons may be elected to take decisions without being thought of as representatives of those who elect them. We used the example of an elected dictator to support this view. How does the executive committee fit in? Is it a representative body? We may consider this question both from the point of view of members and from the point of view of others outside the Club – like its suppliers, potential members, the legal system and so on.

From the point of view of those outside the organization, the committee represents the Club in the important sense that it has the legal power to bind the organization. In a private business venture, or a partnership, or a public limited company, the law confers on some particular individuals the legal power to bind the organization to contractual arrangements. The same applies to this social club: since the members as a whole cannot put their names to a contract to have, say, drinks supplied, particular individuals must be empowered to enter into contractual arrangements for which the assets of the organisation provide an ultimate guarantee. In this simple sense, the committee members represent, or stand for, the group as a whole. The executive members will sign cheques, enter into contractual arrangements and so on, as legal agents of the Club, just as particular individuals will be empowered to bind a large public limited company to a contract, or to draw cheques to meet its obligations. Similarly, if someone wants to make representations to the Club, he or she will turn to the executive in the first instance: for example, someone applying for membership, or a neighbour complaining about noise, will address the committee. In all these cases, the committee represents the Club in its public dealings. (Of course, the situation may be rather more complicated in some ways. For example, the executive may employ a full-time steward and confer some of its powers on that person, so he or she can make commercial arrangements. But this does not alter the point at issue.)

If we now turn to the situation within the Club, the committee represents the group in a rather different way. First, it is the committee's responsibility to enforce the policy and the rules of the Club. Suppose, for example, that a member would like to bring children into the Club on a particular night, when the rules forbid it. In enforcing the rules, the executive committee is employing powers conferred on it by the constitution of the association. Secondly, in as much as the committee makes policy to deal with new circumstances, it may be thought of as representing the members in a different sense: were the members to be expressing a view themselves, what would they conclude? If it is difficult to answer this question, and/or the answer is important (for instance, a developer has made an offer for the Club's premises) the committee members may well decide to use the procedure of the EGM rather than decide themselves. Thirdly, there are circumstances in which the committee would be expected to represent the interests of the Club which are distinct from those in which the legal capacity of its officers is relevant. For example, suppose that a developer has proposed to build a factory on adjacent land: the local press might want to know what the Club thought about the proposal. Although nothing is binding, either in law or as policy, the executive would be expected to take a view on the basis of the interests of the Club, or to guess how its members would feel about the issue.

When we turn to the political system, and focus on national government, there are partial analogies to all these features. Externally, so to speak, other countries or other organizations, like commercial firms, must know who is empowered to bind the state to a particular course of action. For example, the Foreign Secretary usually has the capacity to bind the government, and therefore the country, to particular treaty provisions. Again, ambassadors represent the country in their dealings with foreign governments, or with organizations like the United Nations. Secondly, this representation is not only a matter of the formal, legal, situation, but also a matter of representing interests in negotiation and discussion. Hence the Foreign Office would be expected to have a view about the impact of a proposal by a foreign government on the interests of the nation, just as the executive would be expected to have a view about the interests of the Club in relation to the developer's proposal. Thirdly, just as the executive might be inclined to call an EGM if a new development requires the determination of policy by all the members, so the government might set up a referendum on a new and major issue. (A number of considerations, not least the scale of the operation and its cost, suggest that this route will be less likely to be taken by a national government than a Club committee.)

Internally, similar analogues can be found. The government is empowered to enforce the rules, which in this case refer to law and to the implementation of policy. When a person is prosecuted for a drink-driving offence, if the analogy holds, we should have to suppose that the government is enforcing a decision of the community that drinking and driving is unacceptable behaviour. Again, the government may be thought of as an executive committee, determining policy in the light of new circumstances. For example, before Argentina invaded the Falkland Islands, there had been little public discussion of the appropriate response; but, once the invasion had occurred, some response was obviously required. Pending an opportunity for citizens to make their views known, the government has to represent them, or act on their behalf.

The crucial difference between the Club and the body of citizens, of course, is that there is no AGM in the latter case. There is only an election. For this reason, writers have tried to find in the process of an election features which reproduce *both* the election of an executive committee *and* some equivalent to the AGM itself: in other words, elections are supposed not only to secure the instrumental purpose of electing a body to represent the community until the next election, but also to reproduce the features of an AGM with its expression of popular power and the people's will. (For example, it is this requirement that some public choice theorists have in mind when they compare markets to representative democracy using elections – a comparison we made ourselves in Chapter 2.) In fact, we shall argue, this overburdens elections as a device; they simply cannot fulfil all these different requirements simultaneously. If we care about democracy, it is as important to see what elections cannot achieve (since this directs our attention to other institutional mechanisms which are capable of contributing to the quality of democracy) as it is to ensure that elections are structured to be as democratic as possible. But since we have distinguished between democracy and representative government, we must consider next not the contribution of elections to democracy but the connections between elections and representation. We shall then be in a better position to consider the triadic relations between democracy, representation, and elections.

In the discussion of the analogies between an executive committee and the government, we have left out one level of indirectness, and one important intervening factor. In British electoral practice, voters in individual constituencies vote for a representative; the collection of representatives constitutes a representative assembly, the House of Commons; and the government emerges from the balance of forces in that House. 'Emerges' is not too loose a word: the person invited to form the government, in the usual case, is the leader of the largest party, and the ministers of his or her government are selected in the light of a large number of political considerations.[4] The additional indirectness, compared to our executive committee, exists because of the representative assembly. It is as if the Erewhon members elected a representative committee, from amongst whom officeholders on the executive committee 'emerged'. Hence, although we initially asked in what sense the government might represent the nation or community, we also need to ask in what sense the popular assembly might do so, and also to enquire into the relationship between the assembly and the government.

The intervening factor is the political party. Although there might be factions in the Erewhon Social Club (usually, of course, those who want things to stay as they are and those who want reform), these are not parties. Nevertheless, the existence of factions does raise another question about the representative nature of the executive committee: to what extent does it reflect the relative strength of the factions in the Club? How many factions are there? Are they divided in a cross-cutting way on many different issues, or are there identifiable blocs of opinion lining up in the same way on those different issues?

Our consideration of the relatively simple case of the Erewhon Social Club has enabled us to draw attention to the multiple tasks which elections might be asked to discharge, and to a number of different senses of representation which are relevant to the wider polity[5]. In the following sections we shall consider the implications of this multiplicity of tasks and meanings.

REPRESENTATION

The individual voter, the member and the constituency

An MP is elected in a particular constituency if he or she receives a plurality of votes cast, which, as we know, need not be a majority of votes cast. We may therefore distinguish between the MP as a representative of someone who voted for him or her, someone who voted for another candidate, and someone who did not vote although entitled to do so. Analytically, there is also the person who had no entitlement to vote, who might in some sense be represented, but we leave this aside.

The MP who received the individual's vote

We would expect to find the strongest sense of representation in this case, but it may still be uncertain in exactly what way the MP represents the voter until we know why he or she received the voter's support. (We are leaving aside the question of voting for a government at the moment.) The paradigm case of the MP representing the voter is one in which the voter's political judgements exactly coincide with the candidate's. We may then say that the MP represents the values, opinions and preferences of the voter.

As we move away from the paradigm case, matters are less straightforward. A voter may vote for a candidate not because his or her judgements coincide with the candidates on all issues, but because across a package of policy disputes the candidate's position most nearly corresponds to the voter's: most nearly, that is, of the candidates actually standing. (This problem of the 'package' is an example of what public choice theorists refer to as the problem of 'full-line supply'.[6]) At the level of policy preferences, it does not follow that the MP has the same views on all issues, or indeed on any issue, as the voter. Given the unlikelihood that most voters can cast a vote for someone with whom they are in exact agreement, the argument that MPs represent the policy preferences of even those of their constituents who voted for them is necessarily weak. In addition, we should remember that a voter may support a policy on grounds other than those held by the candidate advocating it.

But there may be other reasons for choosing an MP than coincidence of policy preference. Two of these reasons yield further notions of representation. First, the MP may represent the voter by being the same sort of person, the voter judging that a similar person will have similar interests and opinions. For example, the candidate may share the occupational, class or gender characteristics of the voter. The representation here is based on the idea that the MP, sharing these characteristics with the voter, will use his or her power in the same way as the voter would, if he or she could be present. Secondly, the MP may represent the voter because the voter has most confidence in his or her judgement – a confidence which might well exist without shared characteristics. In this case, the voter need not make policy judgements; he or she needs only to decide who looks best equipped to make them on his or her behalf. I do not have to be a legal expert to decide which lawyer will represent me adequately in court. A final reason for supporting a Parliamentary candidate (but one in which there is no idea of representation) occurs when a voter casts a vote for that candidate solely because he or she is opposing another candidate who is anathema to the voter.

The MP and the voter who voted for another candidate

Barring the case in which voters are very badly informed, and therefore make a mistake in not voting for a candidate who in fact has the characteristics they seek, it is obviously implausible to suppose that the MP represents those who voted for other candidates, in the senses discussed above. In fact, as we shall now see, any sense in which the MP represents those who voted for someone else appears also to be a sense in which the MP represents those who did not vote at all. This attenuates the connection between elections and representation, if not that between democracy and elections.

Representation of those who did not vote

If the MP lives in the constituency there is one sense in which he or she is typical of all three groups (pro-voters, other voters and non-voters): he or she is from the locality. Again, of course, this point does not take us very far, because in Britain many MPs and local councillors do not live in their constituencies or wards. Secondly, even if it were true, an election is not necessary to secure this sort of representativeness. Thirdly, living in an area is a weak sense of typicality; it says nothing about whether the candidate is similar to his or her constituents in any other of the ways that may be important to local life.

Voters' concern with typicality has been a problem for political parties in two obvious ways. First, Scottish Office and Welsh Office ministers have usually been chosen from MPs sitting for Welsh and Scots constituencies. Secondly, parties which have put up 'unconnected' candidates in by-elections have suffered setbacks as voters sometimes reject a candidate with insufficient local connections. (In by-elections, far more attention is likely to be paid to local issues than in a general election.)

So, although it may be empirically true that voters care about local credentials, and that voters can express that concern when the candidates' credentials are in fact different, it is not elections that secure this sort of representativeness but residence qualifications. An election may allow voters to decide how important local connections are, in relation to other considerations, but an election is neither necessary nor sufficient to secure this sort of representativeness.

Another sense of representation which applies to all three groups concerns the role of an MP in looking after the interests of individual constituents who need help. An MP can represent a constituent in dealings with both local and national government. There are many (almost) apolitical cases in which individual constituents need help to secure a fair hearing, and there is no reason to suppose that the availability or quality of this representation could depend upon how, if at all, the constituent voted. (Although, in the absence of a secret ballot, 'punishing' one's opponents by not helping them might be a useful weapon.) When the issue is more clearly political, however, matters will be different. Local concerns can often cut across support for national party positions: in a planning dispute, for example, residents of a locality with quite different party allegiances may oppose a development supported by an equally diverse group. The prudent MP is likely to be agnostic in these cases. A second common case arises from group, rather than individual, interests. If the MP shares the opinions of the group, or is typical of them, then his or her support is likely to be more forthcoming, especially if the issue is important to a substantial number of his or her supporters. So although an MP is capable of representing the individual interests of all constituents in a limited range of cases, group interests are more likely to be pursued by an MP who shares them or sympathizes with them. This is one of the reasons why interest groups of women and ethnic minorities have argued in favour of their being more women and non-white MPs.

We have identified a number of ways in which we can consider the representation of constituents by MPs. In sum, these are (1) shared policy preferences, (2) typicality, either of social characteristics like class, or of locality, (3) representation of interests, either individual or group, and (4) representing someone by making judgements on his or her behalf. We have seen that there is only a limited connection between elections and these different sorts of representativeness. This is because few voters, even those who vote for a particular candidate, will have exactly the same preference profile; because elections are not the only way in which typicality might be secured; and because elections are not the only way to authorize someone to make judgements for you. We have also seen that MPs may be thought to represent all their constituents in some ways, which are independent of the result of the election (except in the sense, of course, that the election points out the person who is to be the representative).

The representative assembly

Social science is familiar with many instances of problems of aggregation – problems which arise when we move from the individual level to the collective level.[7] Electoral systems are themselves mechanisms for aggregating individual choices, made by voters, into collective outcomes, and a lot of the interest and importance of thinking about electoral systems derives from the attempt to work out how exactly the results of aggregation relate to the individual case. There is a similar problem about representation. Given the relations between the individual representative, the MP, and his or her various constituents, what is the relation between the aggregate of MPs, who constitute the House of Commons, and the aggregation of voters, the electorate as a whole?

We may acknowledge immediately that there are some senses of representation under which, *if* each MP were truly a representative of his or her constituency or constituents, then the aggregate of MPs would be a true representative of the country or electorate. As we shall see, there are some limited ways in which this possibility is realized. The more interesting question is this. Since there are limitations upon the ability of any one MP to represent a particular constituency, in what ways are the problems worsened, and in what ways are they diminished, by the process of aggregation? Are there additional opportunities for the assembly to be representative, or does aggregation merely exacerbate the difficulties already identified at the constituency level? What we want to establish are the ways in which the assembly is representative of the country *because* individual MPs are representative of their constituencies, and the ways in which the assembly is representative *despite* individual MPs *not* being so.

The most obvious case of aggregation maintaining representation concerns territory. Since each MP represents a particular geographical area, provided that some MP represents every part of the country, the assembly will represent the territorial jurisdiction. Although the idea that every part of the territory (or, at least, every part of Great Britain and Northern Ireland) should be represented has not been controversial, many other aspects of constituency definition have been. What is the proper size of the territorial unit? Should it be thought of in merely geographical terms, so that any particular square mile is just the same as any other when constituency boundaries are drawn up? Or should constituences have some socio-economic coherence? How should we deal with varying density of settlement? If each constituency has the same territorial size, they will certainly not encompass equal populations.

A second way in which the assembly can maintain the relation between an MP and the constituents concerns authorization. *If* it is plausible to think of an MP as having been authorized to act on behalf of his or her constituents (not simply those who voted in favour), then the assembly has been authorized by the nation. The significance of this depends very much on the constitutional role of the assembly and on the powers that it actually possesses. An assembly holding the powers which direct democracy would claim for the people as a whole, such as the determination of legislation and policy, constitutional amendment, election of the government and so on, might be said to represent the will of the people or popular sovereignty.[8] This is one way in which elections have been seen as devices which enable the ideals of direct democracy to be met despite the impracticalities of assembling the whole people in a large nation state. In relation to the example of the Erewhon Social Club, the analogy would be that the government corresponds to the executive committee, while the assembly corresponds to the AGM – and not that the assembly corresponds to the executive committee. The assembly would then be treated as if it were an assembly of the people, possessing the people's powers conveyed to it through the electoral process of representation.

For many reasons, of course, such a model does not correspond to the realities of British politics. First, constitutionally, the Queen in Parliament is sovereign, rather than the people or the House of Commons acting on their behalf. Consequently, neither legislation nor policy is solely determined by the popular assembly. Of course, to decide the precise scope of the Commons' actual powers would require a close analysis of what actually happens, rather than of the constitutional position; but we can certainly say that the House of Commons does not have the legislative and policy-making powers the model requires. Secondly, the assembly does not elect a government. The government emerges from the balance of forces in the assembly, and, as we shall see below, general elections are regarded as a device linking voters directly to the choice of a government. (On this other model, the government still corresponds to the executive committee, but the assembly no longer corresponds to the AGM.) The representative assembly does have the power to bring down a government, however, and so the continuing tenure of any particular government does require the support of the assembly.[9] Thirdly, individual MPs are not delegated or mandated by their constituents in the way this model would require, because the idea of the mandate has been invoked only in a limited way to suggest that voters may give an opinion to their MPs about policies. We may contrast this with the idea that the assembly is a collection of delegates who have been instructed how to vote on issues after discussion and voting by those whom they represent.

When we consider representation at this aggregate level, then, geographical aggregation and collective authorization are two limited ways in which the representativeness of a particular MP with respect to a particular constituency might be translated into the representativeness of the assembly with respect to the nation. They are limited ways because geographical representation is a weak sense of the concept, and because of the limited plausibility in current practice of supposing that all voters in a constituency authorize the MP who is elected to serve it. Let us now turn, instead, to what we might call countervailing discrepancies in representation: to the idea that the assembly could be representative of the nation as a whole even if, and perhaps because, individual MPs do not represent all their constituents.

One set of possibilities relies on the idea that the assembly is a microcosm of the nation in some specified way, so that each elector is represented by someone in the assembly. It is obvious, though, that there is an infinite number of possible characteristics of the general population, so some have to be picked out as politically significant. To be frivolous, no-one has proposed that the assembly should contain the same proportion of redheaded persons as the general population; but, to be serious, the small number of MPs who are not white, who are not men, who are not university graduates, and, one might add, who are not members of a political party has drawn criticism. Different arguments favouring a particular characteristic will have to be backed up by an explanation of its significance. And usually, this explanation will suggest that there are groups in society whose interests will be neglected unless they are represented in the assembly in similar proportions to their incidence in the wider community.

It is important to see, however, that this argument relies on two steps, and that the connection between them has been the subject of great controversy. It is possible to accept that the assembly should be a microcosm of the community, to take this to mean that all interests in the community should have representation, and to deny that this requires any correspondence between the proportion of representatives associated with that interest and the proportion of persons in the community who possess it. At the extreme, it could be held that one farmer in the House of Commons will represent the farming interest, that there is no need for 3 per cent of MPs to be farmers. Is the aim to give every interest a voice, or a proportion of voices in the assembly which corresponds to the strength of the interest in the community?

It is worth emphasizing the difficulties of associating territorial constituencies with the representation of many sorts of interest. Functional representation, the representation of particular interest blocs, is usually excluded by the constituency system unless there happens to be a high level of correspondence between the distinctiveness of local socio-economic characteristics and the characteristics highlighted for attention. (This problem is explored further in Chapter 6.) There are no constituencies with a large proportion of women voters, although there are constituencies with a high proportion of non-middle-class voters. Historically, it was not implausible for the MP from Bristol to be thought of as representing a shipping and trading interest, and the MP from Manchester to represent manufacturing; but most of these associations no longer hold (Beer 1969: 71–2).

A second objection to the proportional interpretation of the microcosm may be put as a question. If the idea is to protect a certain sort of interest, need the representative personally share it, or is it sufficient that he or she be elected by those who do? For example, does the representation of the poor, or pensioners, require that some poor persons or retired people sit in Parliament, or is it sufficient that they are electors? If no-one is excluded from the franchise, the electorate is the community, and the job of taking account of all interests is tackled by universal suffrage.

The argument that universal franchise is insufficient to achieve representation claims that the system of aggregating votes employed (through plurality voting in constituencies) systematically favours some at the expense of others, and that proper representation requires not only universal suffrage but also an assembly which is a microcosm of the electorate. This argument may refer both to the difficulty some interests will experience in mobilizing at all, and to biases in the electoral system which disfavour them. Historically, these arguments have turned on class: it was the aim of the Labour Representation Committee to get representatives sympathetic to the working class (even if not themselves members of it) into Parliament, not merely to get working men the vote (Ensor 1936: 265–6). At the present day, the argument concerns party political orientation: the House of Commons should contain MPs of each party in proportion to the total number of votes cast for that party in the election. In this sense, the proportional microcosm argument is being used as a criticism of plurality voting. This particular criticism, however, should be treated with caution, because there are circumstances in which a plurality system may achieve greater proportionality between party support and the composition of the assembly than supposedly 'proportional' voting systems.

We can now see, then, that there are two arguments which suggest that the assembly is truly representative even if the relation between an MP and his or her constituents is not. The first relies simply on the fact of aggregation: if there is universal franchise, the assembly is the result of all views and opinions. This is a weak argument, because put like this it is merely definitional: it does not rely on any systematic connection between the views and opinions and the composition of the assembly. Without such a connection, it maintains that one is represented if one participated, or even merely could have participated, in an election. The second argument suggests a mechanism: diverse constituencies will elect diverse representatives, so all interests will be represented. For example, suppose a predominantly working class constituency will choose a working class member, while a predominantly middle class constituency will choose a middle class member. The working class minority in the latter constituency, and the middle class minority in the former constituency, will still have a sort of representation, in terms of interests, but not one provided by their local MPs. Hence aggregation helps to make up for the defects in the plurality system at constituency level. The argument is not very convincing. The problems are first, that it relies on all relevant interests being determinant in some constituency (which is highly implausible); secondly, that it concedes the need to represent socially diverse interests, but maintains a commitment to constituency-based voting; and thirdly that it denies the need to represent not only the existence but also the strength of an interest group.

Representation and the election of governments

A voter in a British general election knows that the results of the election, overall, will be used to determine which party (in the usual case) will form the incoming government. But since any new government is selected by the Prime Minister, the voter does not have advance information about the composition of a potential government. The voter knows only the leaders of particular parties, and therefore who is likely to be Prime Minister if that party 'wins' the election. In relation to the government, then, the voter can be taken to be expressing a preference only about the party which will form it, and/or a judgement or preference about which party leader should be Prime Minister. The voter is not presented with rival slates of candidates for specific offices, and therefore will not suffer the long-ballot fatigue mentioned in Chapter 3, but with packages of policies associated with particular parties and their leaders.

This package is presented to the electorate as a manifesto, a statement of the content of policies, and sometimes the priorities among them, that the party would pursue in power. Because these manifestos have been put before voters at the time of the election, it has suited governments to claim that they have a mandate to pursue those policies when in office. In other words, from the government's point of view, the election is taken to be a direct judgement of preferred policies, licensing their implementation by the successful party. Once again, we find an element in direct democracy – voting on policy proposals – being 'read into' the electoral procedures of indirect democracy. We should therefore compare the two situations, and ask whether the claim to a mandate is sustainable, and what its limits are.

Two crucial differences between direct democracy and indirect democracy will be obvious. First, in a direct democracy, there is no reason to vote on packages of proposals: each may be taken separately. The aggregation of policies into a platform, the creation of a manifesto, limits the assumptions that can be made about the voters' preferences, as we shall see below. Secondly, in a direct democracy a proposal is usually passed when a majority of voters favour it. In the British system, there is no logical reason why the largest party in the House of Commons, which will form the government, should have received more votes than the second largest party – and in 1951 and February 1974 it did not. It is not, therefore, necessarily true that the largest party received a majority of votes, or even a plurality of votes, although it may happen that way. In any case, the fact that policy information was provided in a manifesto does not entail that voters took it into account. The combination of these points severely limits any claim that the electorate has mandated the government to pursue all the policies contained in its manifesto.

If policy proposals can be taken individually, we would expect a greater correspondence between voters' preferences and policies adopted than would exist if policies are aggregated. Although this comparison could become very complicated if we take account of intensities of preference, the expectation relies on a simple intuition. If voters have to vote on a package of policies, they may have to vote in favour of a proposal which they would reject if it were separately discussed. All that a particular vote in favour of a package can be taken to mean is that, for that voter, the package on balance was preferable to any other package on offer. The situation is similar to purchasing a complex consumer good. Even in a competitive market, all consumers can do is to choose the product that on balance has more of the features they seek than any other. But this does not mean that the product reflects all the single-choice preferences of a particular consumer; the consumer may 'settle' for something which is suitable in the most important respects, even if it is does not have other desired features (such as a favoured colour). And if that is true in a relatively competitive market, it is of course even more likely to be true in an oligopolistic one.

The point here is not that trade-offs between different considerations should be avoidable in a perfect market. The point, rather, is what may be legitimately inferred from a choice once it is made. Just as we do not know that a consumer is perfectly satisfied with some product purchased, only that it came nearest of what was on offer to what was required, so we do not know that a voter who casts a vote for a package of policies is in favour of any particular one of them. Hence although a government might truly claim that its pre-election manifesto presented a package that a plurality of voters favoured, it could not truly claim that each policy in it had such support.

Clearly, then, the idea that the government has received a mandate cannot be taken to mean that every policy, taken singly, would receive the number of votes that the governing party received. It might be more or less. Another way of looking at the mandate doctrine would take this into account. Now the claim is not about individual policies, but entitlement to govern. The government has been elected by fair procedures, and the election confers legitimacy on its acts. The role of the manifesto, in this view, would be to assist in the process of accountability rather than to enable citizens to express policy preferences. The parties lay out their proposals, and once they are implemented the electorate can see their impact and take that into account in a future election.

We shall have cause to return to the relationship between election results, policy proposals and legitimacy in subsequent chapters, when we take up two features of the British system in more detail. These are its use of plurality voting and its territorial base. Both of these features are relevant to the issues surrounding the mandate and legitimacy. We shall be asking whether the claim to a mandate might be stronger with a different voting procedure, and whether, under plurality voting, strong regional patterns of party support weaken the claim of a government to a national mandate. This question will be discussed in Chapter 6. For the present, we may simply note that the claim to legitimacy conferred by an election does not require any reference to policies. The incumbents will necessarily face new issues and new difficulties when in power, and their authority to deal with them can be derived directly from their having been elected, without reference to the content of the manifesto. A party might have the confidence of the electorate even if the voters do not know about the content of its policies.

If claims to a mandate are to be taken seriously, they require at the very least a negative corollary: that no important policy may be introduced unless it has been put forward to the electorate.

There have been occasions on which such a view has been adopted. But these have been more nearly single-issue elections than is usually the case, and the limits of the mandate still have to be recognized. For example, the elections called by Asquith were fought on the proper extent of the powers of the House of Lords, and it eventually became clear that a majority of those who voted wished them to be limited (Ensor 1936: 418). It was entirely plausible, within the limits of the plurality system, to claim a mandate for reform. Three points should be made about the negative corollary. First, the definition of an *important* policy could be contentious: the Asquith example is one in which it was broadly agreed that constitutional issues were at stake. Secondly, the most appropriate mechanism for determining the electorate's view of a single issue is the referendum. Thirdly, the negative corollary can provide only a weak safeguard; it does not, in a multi-issue election, provide any guarantee that the policy is acceptable to all who vote for the party.

Can we say, then, that the government represents the electorate? Since the governing party receives the votes of only a portion of that electorate, it seems unlikely. In fact, the partial character of government increases the need for a representative assembly, in which the interests of those who did not support the incumbents can at least be expressed. Our discussion of the manifesto–mandate doctrine further suggests that the government cannot claim that any particular policy is supported even by as many people as voted for it. We have argued that it is more plausible to think of the government being authorized to act by the electoral process, that elections confer legitimacy, than that elections under the British system can convey sufficient information about voters' policy preferences to license the claim that the government's policies represent what the electorate wants.

Despite these reservations about the government's claim to represent the population, as an internal relation, it is, of course, true that the government represents the nation in some external respects. When negotiations in foreign affairs are in progress, when the EEC is discussing common measures against terrorism or football hooliganism, the government acts for the electorate and is treated by other participants as the true representative of the country. Three aspects of this are worthy of note. The first reverts to the notions of legitimacy and authorization discussed earlier: the government can be treated as the representative of the nation because the electoral process has conferred legitimacy upon it, that is the outcome of the electoral process is treated as sufficient evidence of the government's entitlement to act on behalf of citizens. Secondly, in these external relations, the government is thought to be pursuing a public or national interest. For example, in trying to agree with other European nations on measures for pollution control, the government is forwarding the public interest in a healthy environment. When it is engaged in discussions about military arrangements, it is concerned with a national interest. We shall see below that our view of the electoral system will rest heavily on which institutions and processes we think are in principle capable of dealing with conflicts of interests in domestic politics. The third point concerns representation conceived symbolically. The Head of State is representative in this symbolic sense. Some Heads of State, like the American President, are also heads of the executive branch of government; others, like the British monarch, are not.

ELECTIONS, DEMOCRACY AND REPRESENTATION: ASPECTS OF AGGREGATION

In a direct democracy, it is tempting to think that the public interest is what the 'the people' say it is. After all, if there is an opportunity for debate, if everyone can make proposals to the group, if all can vote on those proposals, then surely the 'public interest' is what emerges from those processes. The whole procedure is an aggregation process, made necessary by the need for common action or a common decision. But what exactly is aggregated?

The answer to this question determines the weight we want to attach to the result. Rousseau, for example, made a distinction between the general will and the will of all. No doubt this distinction contains many obscurities, but its central point seems plain enough (Rousseau 1913: 23; Riley 1986: 241–60). Let us consider the concrete example of the referendum on Britain's continued membership of the EEC. As an individual voter, I could ask myself (1) is such membership in my interests, or (2) is such membership in the interests of all citizens (including myself)? If we aggregate the votes cast when individuals answer these questions, the significance of the result is quite different. Suppose a majority answer the first question positively. Then we have aggregated judgements about individual interests; we know that more people think they will benefit than think they will disbenefit. The voting system is responsible for reporting the interests of individuals. Suppose that the second question is answered positively by a majority. More people judge that membership is in everyone's interest than do not. Now voters are undertaking a sort of aggregation exercise before they cast their vote: they are trying to take everyone into account. The result of such a vote is an aggregation of individual judgements about the aggregate effects of a policy. Rousseau thought that this second sort of aggregation had greater moral force than the first, that it indicated the general will rather than the will of all, and that the will of all should not be the basis for action because it was selfishly motivated.

Whether or not Rousseau's treatment of these matters was coherent, the question he was raising is crucial to our thinking about electoral systems and representation. It was because those devices were unable to sustain the moral purity of the general will that Rousseau was so dismissive of the representation of sovereignty (1913: 20). The question for us is whether representative government is capable of expressing anything like the general will, or the public interest, and the role of aggregation and representation in that process. More particularly, is a voter at election time expressing a view about which party would provide best for his or her interests, or expressing a view about which government can best pursue the public interest? Are election results indicators of who will do well out of particular policies, or judgements about which party will do best for us as a whole?

Theories of democracy, in both its direct and its representative forms, have been troubled by reconciling their underlying claims to political equality with the dangers of majority rule (Mill 1910: 256–76; Lively 1975: 25–7). That is, political equality requires that all interests are taken into account, that all have an equal influence on the result; but if democracy means only rule by the majority, it enables the majority to prosper at the expense of the minority. Recognition of this simple fact has usually led to advocacy of other mechanisms or safeguards to protect the interests of the minority. Rousseau's hopes for a moralized citizenry are just one form of such safeguards – another example is the constitutional provision of a bill of rights. In relation to British indirect democracy, if we assume that the government is voted in by a majority who hope it will serve their personal interests, then it may well be the government that needs to be restrained in the name of the minority it does not represent. This is a role theoretically performed by an assembly which is supposed to represent everyone. Some governments are more sensitive than others to the consideration that they do not enjoy universal support, but the growing tendency to rely on a defective doctrine of the mandate gives little ground for optimism. Under alternative indirect systems, accommodation between different interest groups may occur in the process of coalition government formation, but of course these alternatives do not employ the plurality voting system.

The reconciliation of interests in a representative system might, then, be put in the hands of voters, might be an expectation of the assembly, might occur in government formation, or be attempted in the process of policy formation. If it is hoped that the assembly could contribute to interest reconciliation, then the microcosm notion of representation seems to be required: the balance of forces in the assembly should reflect the balance of interests in the community. Of course, the assembly needs a voting rule, and the microcosm approach will not by itself prevent self-interested majoritarian legislation. The problem of institutional design here, however, is to minimize a defect. Even if the government represents the interests of a majority, the minority will be better served by an assembly which represents its true numbers.

CONCLUSION

In this chapter, we have looked at many different roles the electoral system has been assigned by those who see it as a vital component of a democratic system. It is a familiar truth that a tool designed to do many jobs may not do any of them particularly well. Two major conclusions follow from this. The first is that claims about what the electoral system 'reveals' should be treated with great scepticism. The second is that even if there are limits to what can be conveyed by elections, we ought not to be indifferent to where those limits come, and we ought to try to compensate for the limitations of the electoral system in other areas of our political practice. (For example, we might try to overcome defects in one area of interest reconciliation, identified above, in another area.)

We may conclude by reviewing those multiple roles, their relation to democracy, and the levels of aggregation involved. In a direct democracy, outcomes follow from an aggregation of voters' opinions or judgements – about policy, law or common action of some kind. These judgements may be based on a consideration of self-interest or general interest. This sort of direct democracy is defended by reference to ideals of self-government, popular sovereignty, participation and political equality. Representative government is pragmatically defended as the nearest practical approach to direct democracy, and hence the electoral arrangements are supposed to embody, as far as possible, the democratic ideals. Instead of literal self-rule, it is rule by those chosen by the people; instead of continuous participation in policy formation, it provides an opportunity to express opinions as far as is practicable; universal franchise contributes to popular sovereignty. The electoral system is thus a surrogate for direct democracy, and votes are interpreted as views about policies.

But representative government, as constituted in Britain, brings with it other possibilities. An election 'selects' a Prime Minister, and the party of government. It makes the rulers accountable to the people. It is taken to legitimize the use of political power. An election also determines individual representatives, and the composition of the representative assembly. The problem of aggregation, under this practice, is quite different from that in direct democracy. First, voters are faced with a package of policies, not individual decisions – the policies themselves are aggregated. Secondly, individual MPs are chosen by aggregating votes in particular constituencies. Thirdly, the representative assembly is an aggregation of individual MPs. Fourthly, the government emerges as a consequence of the composition of the representative assembly. The electorate *as a whole* is in effect choosing particular individuals to be representatives, the composition of the representative assembly, the person who is to be Prime Minister, and a package of policies associated with a particular party. But this is a statement of the consequences of individuals' casting votes: it is wholly metaphysical to think of the electorate actually choosing all these things. As a result, the meaning of even an individual vote, and certainly of the aggregation of votes, is always unclear. It does not follow from the fact that the voter could have made one of these consequences of his or her vote the determining one that he or she did so.

From a more abstract theoretical point of view, the contrast here can be expressed in a nutshell. In a direct democracy, with single-issue voting and no parties, the results of voting reveal which policies are favoured (for whatever reason) by how many people.[10] In the British system of representative government, by contrast, any one vote can be interpreted in terms of any of the consequences to which it contributes. But the more consequences a vote has, the less information it conveys, because we do not know which particular reasons were operative for any one voter. Now the problem is not only the motivational one, present in direct democracy. It is the limits of legitimate inference from a vote to support for a particular individual, particular party, particular government, or particular policy. By giving the electoral system so much to do simultaneously, we limit the conclusions we can draw from its results.

In the next chapter, we shall consider arguments suggesting that the voter's motive will depend, at least in part, on the form of the ballot. We shall be considering the advantages and disadvantages of voting openly and in secret. In Chapter 6 we explore in greater detail the territorial dimension of elections, a dimension which we have discussed in this chapter in relation to problems of representation. We shall then be able to move on to a comparison between the plurality system and alternatives to it.

5   Secret and open voting

INTRODUCTION

This chapter considers the connection between the act of voting and the requirements of secrecy or publicity surrounding that act. Throughout the book, we have been concerned not only with comparisons between different electoral systems, but also with using examples drawn from voting systems which do not necessarily have electing officeholders as their objective. For example, votes are taken to determine policy. In Chapter 4, we discussed the contrast between representative government and democracy, and we saw that the most obvious contrast between the two was the highly attenuated connection, in the former, between citizens' votes and policy determination. The differences between direct and indirect democracy will prove to be important in our consideration of the connection between democracy and secrecy, and thus in the more specific context of secrecy in electoral systems. In Chapter 3, we saw that whether the ballot is secret or not is a major, but often neglected, aspect of one of the three 'phases' of an electoral system, namely ballot structure.

It falls to political scientists to explore aspects of political practice which may be taken for granted (at least today) by others. Just as, we argued, 'one person, one vote' is a commonly accepted (but inadequate) conception of democracy, so the idea that democracy necessarily requires a secret ballot is a widely held assumption. Both these notions have a particular history, and were certainly not always subscribed to generally. In the nineteenth century, there were major debates about the desirability of a secret ballot – often called simply the ballot – not only in Britain, but also in other emergent liberal democracies, such as the United States. The significance of examining arguments in favour of a secret ballot does not depend solely, however, on the fact that this was once a contentious issue. If we consider voting and decision-making in contexts other than representative government, it is far from clear that secrecy is desirable. For example, consider the profound differences in the practice of trial by jury which would result from a requirement that jurors vote secretly, even when deliberating, on the question of the accused's guilt. More generally, we should beware of transplanting arguments from one context into another too readily – just as, we have seen, we should beware of assuming that arguments supporting 'one person, one vote' are defensible in all circumstances. (Sometimes, weighted votes are fairer.)

Our enquiry, then, is addressed to the question: does democracy, and hence representative government, require openness or secrecy in the voting system? Our characterization of democracy associated it with political equality and participation, general values which, we saw, imply particular procedures: the opportunity to make proposals to the group, the opportunity to discuss them, equality in votes when a decision is taken and so on. Although representative government provides for these values in only a weakened form, political equality and participation can still be used as yardsticks by which to assess the procedures peculiar to it: for example, everyone should have the same number of votes and the opportunity to vote should be distributed fairly. It makes sense, then, to use the ideals of political equality and participation in an assessment of the demands of secrecy or openness in voting systems.

We should remind ourselves first, however, that the modern association between democracy and secrecy is exactly that. Legislation to require secret balloting in Parliamentary and local elections in Britain was passed only in 1872 – sixteen years after it was first used in Australia. A hundred years may be a long time, but Parliament claimed to represent the people long before the secret ballot was introduced. And democracy (rather than representative government) was associated with public discussion and public voting. The next section explores the distinction between voting as a public act and voting as a private act, a distinction insisted upon in a famous argument against the secret ballot put forward by John Stuart Mill in 1861. Our aim is to draw out the aspects of the contrast between 'the public' and the 'private' which are involved in democratic voting. The following section discusses the relationship between secrecy and serial (as against simultaneous) voting. We shall want to refer back to the arguments surrounding the Ballot Act to establish why secrecy was thought to be necessary, and in the subsequent two sections of the chapter we shall be reviewing some arguments for and against secrecy.

JOHN STUART MILL ON VOTING AS A PUBLIC ACT

Mill expressed his opposition to the secret ballot in *Considerations on Representative Government*:

> In any political election, even by universal suffrage (and still more obviously in the case of a restricted suffrage), the voter is under an absolute moral obligation to consider the interest of the public, not his private advantage, and give his vote to the best of his judgment, exactly as he would be bound to do if he were the sole voter, and the election depended upon him alone. This being admitted, it is at least a *prima facie* consequence that the duty of voting, like any other public duty, should be performed under the eye and criticism of the public; every one of whom has not only an interest in its performance, but a good title to consider himself wronged if it is performed otherwise than honestly and carefully.
>
> (Mill 1910: 300)

It is clear from this that Mill's opposition rests on a particular theory of representative government, and this makes it worth thinking about the contrasts he draws in relation to theories of democracy enunciated long after he was writing.[1] In his own time, Mill was considered to be radical in his attachment to representative government, since he advocated, to a derisive House of Commons, the enfranchisement of women.[2] His essay provides a classic defence of the practice of representative government, so his opposition to the secret ballot is especially striking.

His central point is that voting is necessarily a public act, because a vote is a contribution to a result which will commit the group to an outcome binding it collectively. This point is most obvious in direct democracy, when policy is determined by the voting procedure. Its application to representative government, for Mill, was that the choice of a representative had important consequences for the use of public power. His account does not mention political parties of the modern kind, and the role of the voter, for him, was to choose the representative who was best able to secure the general happiness. The voter expressed a particular judgement about the candidate most likely to secure (what we would now call) the public interest.

In this way, Mill adopted the position previously held by both Rousseau and Condorcet, but two contrasts with many modern theories are immediately obvious. First, the contemporary voter (in Britain) has to take account of party and party leadership. Perhaps Mill's prescription would then be that the voter should support that party or leader most able to secure the general happiness. Secondly, Mill's theory requires the voter to calculate the impact of a politician on the general happiness. Many modern theories suppose, by contrast, that the voter should examine the impact of the politician on his own utility, narrowly defined.[3]

It was precisely this concern with private interest which Mill associated with the secret ballot:

> bad voting is now less to be apprehended from the influences to which the voter is subject at the hands of others, than from the sinister interests and discreditable feelings which belong to himself, either individually or as a member of a class. To secure him against the first at the cost of removing all restraint from the last, would be to exchange a smaller and diminishing evil for a greater and increasing one.
>
> (Mill 1910: 301)

Mill obviously acknowledges the dangers of influence (and coercion) but he regards that as a lesser evil than selfish or ill-considered voting. We shall later want to consider whether we accept his judgement.

Underlying Mill's opposition to the secret ballot is the profoundly held belief, expressed in the first quotation, that the possession of the vote brings with it *moral* obligations to the rest of the community. This argument is not heard much these days, so it may be elaborated a little here. Thinking of the radical theories of the eighteenth century, in particular, Mill identified a class of claims about democracy which he thought were based on error. This type of claim to democracy treated the vote as a *right*, thus encouraging the voter to believe he possessed the vote in order to benefit himself. The true position, according to Mill, was that he possessed it as a *trust*, that it was designed to benefit all, and that he was accountable to others for the use to which he put it. This is why he distinguished, in the first quotation, between the position of the voter under universal suffrage and under a more restricted franchise. The responsibility to others was heightened if those others had no vote; but universal franchise did not remove it.

The antithesis of Mill's position is expressed by the voter who refuses to discuss how he or she used the ballot, claiming that it is private and that others should mind their own business. As we shall see in more detail later, debates about whether votes should be taken openly or in secret reveal different attitudes to the question of whether the way we vote (in any circumstances) should be regarded as merely our own business.

SIMULTANEOUS AND SERIAL VOTING: THE ROLE OF IGNORANCE

In addition to the distinction between secret and public acts of voting, we should consider another distinction, to which it is related. That is, the distinction between *simultaneous* and *serial* methods of expressing an opinion. In ice-skating competitions, for example, the judges are required to display their marks for each competitor at a given signal, so they all state their judgements at the same time. One reason for this, obviously, is that the procedure makes it impossible for any particular judge to hold back, waiting to see what others think and allowing their opinion to influence the marks he or she awards. In other words, the procedure insists on independent judgements by enforcing simultaneity.

In other contexts, the point of the voting procedure may be to produce a collective judgement. For example, a jury composed of twelve persons is required, at least initially, to try to come to a common view about the guilt of the accused. It is very unlikely that this initial unanimity requirement will be met without the opportunity for discussion. Although the independent judgement of each juror is valued, and is reflected in each juror's initial veto power over the collective decision, the procedure seeks a common view with which each juror is independently satisfied. A jury foreman chairing the discussion is likely to start by taking a straw poll; and if the foreman is aware of the point in view here, he or she will ask for a (simultaneous) show of hands by which the immediate opinions of the different jurors can be gauged. If there are two opinion blocs, discussion can then begin on the reasons each has for the particular view he or she adopts. And this discussion is aimed at producing a unanimous view. Such a two stage process will encourage the integrity of the first opinion (insulating any juror from an inclination to 'go with the crowd' rather than express his or her own opinion) while allowing for the proper influence of other jurors, through argument and reasoning rather than weight of numbers.

The relationship between simultaneity and secrecy is, then, clear. Instead of a simultaneous show of hands, the jurors could write their immediate opinions on a piece of paper which is handed to the foreman. Secrecy provides a means to achieve the same results as a simultaneous expression of views, independence, even if the votes are cast serially, because each voter votes in ignorance of what the other voters have done or will do. Given our characterisation of the basic features of democracy, this is a crucial point. It has several aspects, which we may consider in turn.

First, there is a difference between voting in ignorance of other voters' actions, and never knowing how they voted. As we have seen, some mechanisms which secure the former result also produce the second. The secret ballot as presently understood, for example, secures both. But simultaneous voting, or secret serial voting, can both secure the first without necessitating the second. Our jury foreman, for example, can announce that six jurors think the defendant is guilty and six think the defendant is innocent. It is then necessary for the respective opinion blocs to be identified so discussion can begin.

Secondly, we can consider the distinction between simultaneous and serial voting, as it has now been developed, from the perspective of the democratic commitment to political equality. There is, of course, a relationship between equality and independence, which now becomes clearer. There are two respects in which voting in ignorance of the votes of others relates to political equality. On the one hand, a concern with equality may make us want to guard against someone 'following the crowd'. If I simply vote the way others do, or if I decide I'll vote as you do, the influence of others on me certainly reduces the independence of my vote. This appears to count against equality in the vote as well – but this appearance actually depends on the motive for adopting someone else's point of view. On the other hand, there is another threat to equality. If we vote serially and openly, later voters know their chances of determining the outcome. This may affect both their propensity to participate, and increase their power. This is because these later voters are placed more like the chairperson of a committee who has a casting vote. Before anyone has voted, his or her casting vote is merely potentially determining, and does not represent additional power. But if there is a tie, the power is very real. So too with later voters. This may not matter, may not undermine equality, if there are a large number of votes and a random ordering of voting. But if the voting order is fixed, there is inequality of power. The following story illustrates these points perfectly:

PUSH-BUTTON THREAT TO ISLAND'S DELIBERATIONS

From Phil Reeves
St Peter Port

One of the more curious ancient customs of Guernsey, in the Channel Islands, is threatened by the computer age.

A move is afoot to change the way votes are cast in the States of Deliberation, the local equivalent of Parliament, whose roots are in the 17th century.

A seasoned Guernsey politician and Methodist minister, Alan Ingrouille, has asked the authorities to introduce American-style push-button voting machines.

The island has no political parties. According to tradition votes are usually cast orally. Those in favour shout 'Pour!'; those against 'Contre!'. Ditherers can abstain by bellowing 'Je ne vote pas!' The loudest element wins. Mr Ingrouille says trouble arises with a recorded vote.

The 55-member States includes a powerful group of 12 *conseillers*, elected by an elite electoral college. Recorded votes are taken in open session one by one and in the same order. The *conseillers* open the batting and considerable power accumulates to those at the end of the queue.

Few in Guernsey have forgotten the occasion, five years ago, when the States tried to introduce universal franchise. The recorded vote was a tie and the bid failed on the Speaker's casting vote. Two members from Alderney, a tiny island 20 miles away, voted last – against change.

The solution, according to Mr Ingrouille, is to install a computer allowing votes to be cast simultaneously. But he wants the buttons marked 'Pour', 'Contre' and 'Je ne vote pas!'

The Independent

Thirdly, voting in ignorance of what others have done, in an election, requires not only secrecy at the polls but some further conditions. No result may be declared in any constituency, for example, before all the polling stations in all constituencies have shut. This requires that the hours for polling be the same in all constituencies. In addition, even exit polls are not published in Britain while the polling stations are still open. These practices are comparatively recent. In many countries, including Britain, Canada, and the United States, it was usual for polling to take place on different occasions in different localities. Even today, when polling takes place on a single day in US presidential elections, the results of the election in the eastern states are being declared while voting booths are still open in the western states. This can have an impact on the votes cast – for example, when there is a landslide victory in the offing, participation rates in the west fall.[4]

Fourthly, we may find there is a conflict between two aspects of the act of voting. On the one hand, insulating the voter from the opinions or judgements of others may increase his or her independence. On the other hand, such an insulation may make it impossible to know how someone voted, and therefore reduce accountability. Consider again the example of the London club which allows existing members to vote on the admission of a new member, using the veto procedure. Members are allowed (secretly) to drop a black ball (signifying a veto) into an urn. Secrecy here allows each member to take an independent view of the applicant; but it also makes it impossible to argue with anyone about the 'reasons' he or she has for exercising the veto. These may be founded in prejudice, gossip or solid fact: but since they do not have to be defended, no-one will ever know what the reason for the veto was.

This is by no means a trivial point related only to social clubs. The same contrast between independence through secrecy, and account-ability, exists when Members of Parliament cast a vote on a legislative proposal. This is a public act: records can be consulted by electors who would wish to hold their representative accountable for what he or she did. But at the same time, this publicness may discourage the MP from making an independent judgement on the merits of the proposed legislation. His/her vote will be publicly recorded, and both constituents and other members of the MP's party will be able to call him/her to account. John Stuart Mill's vision of both the voter and the represent-ative was of the rugged and self-confident individual who would not be deflected from his/her own judgement by the need to justify it to others, or by the inducements of preference. In other words, Mill thought that for strong-minded persons, the need to account for one's actions would not be a threat to independent judgement; indeed, the need to account for oneself would stimulate that strong-minded independence. Contem-porary talk of 'lobby-fodder' is rooted in a less optimistic perception.

Fifthly, we may return to John Stuart Mill's main point. That was that secrecy makes voters more likely to consider the vote something designed to benefit themselves as individuals, rather than something designed to secure the general good. According to Mill, then, something like the general will beloved by Rousseau was more likely to emerge from open voting than from secrecy. For him, the effect of secrecy was to encourage the expression of private interest, and the result of such a procedure could only be Rousseau's will of all (Mill 1910: 298–9). This point will be discussed in further detail in the subsequent two sections.

Finally, secrecy conceived as a requirement of independence has an important bearing on arguments about strategic voting and logrolling. We have already seen that voting later than others, when their votes are known, gives the later voter an advantage. If there is secrecy, or simultaneity, then strategic voting requires that the voter guess how others are going to vote. Both secrecy and simultaneity make successful strategic voting more difficult. Whether or not this is a benefit depends upon how strategic voting is regarded: as a threat to democracy, or as a natural aspect of it.

Just as strategic voting has a disputable place in democratic theory, so too does logrolling. 'Logrolling' refers to the practice of trading votes, so that a person supports a proposal which may have little or no relation to his or her own interests, in order to obtain support from another voter for his or her own objectives. Secret voting makes it difficult for either of the two parties who have promised to trade votes to be sure that the other fulfils its side of the bargain. Hence logrolling works best where there is an open vote. For those who consider logrolling a sophisticated development of democracy, there is a cost to secrecy; for those who think that logrolling is a corruption of the democratic process, secrecy is to be valued. Both a simultaneous vote and a secret vote, on a package of proposals, require the vote traders to trust each other to cast the votes as agreed. An open but simultaneous vote will enable recriminations later, and affect reputations for trustworthiness; but by then the decisions have been made. On the other hand, serial voting on a set of measures requires one party to perform its side of the bargain before the other; and if the first party does vote as agreed, the second has an incentive to ignore the agreement, having already secured its objective. So the ideal situation to encourage logrolling is probably openness rather than secrecy, but simultaneous rather than serial voting. In that way, secrecy discourages logrolling.

Our lengthy preliminary has been concerned with the connections between secret and open voting on the one hand, and simultaneous and serial voting on the other. We have stressed that these connections are various. It is worth noting, before we move on, that one feature of modern society is likely to bring the two distinctions together. That feature is the size of the electorate. As we saw, a reason for secrecy is that secret serial voting reproduces one feature of simultaneous voting – the voter votes in ignorance of how others cast their ballots. Pragmatically, the size of modern electorates makes simultaneous voting impossible. It also precludes reproducing other features of direct democracy, like face to face discussion between all the voters before the ballot, and defence of the use of the ballot afterwards. But even if the size of Parliamentary electorates requires serial voting, and even if serial voting provides a good reason for secrecy, we should not identify democracy with secrecy. Many other voting bodies are much smaller than a Parliamentary constituency, and in the next two sections we shall use examples drawn from such smaller electorates to provide comparisons.

ARGUMENTS FOR OPENNESS

We may now develop two arguments for open voting, and consider their adequacy, their limitations, and their applicability in different contexts. We shall, of course, be particularly concerned with their applicability to electoral competitions. They concern accountability and commitment.

Accountability

If we wish to hold people accountable for the way in which they cast a vote, we obviously need to know how it has been cast. The substantive arguments here are going to concern the appropriateness and desirability of holding someone accountable, rather than any uncertainty about the relation between accountability and openness. We wish for the votes of our MPs to be recorded, so we can examine their record and see to what extent they agree with us, or we agree with them. (The amount of information available to voters has varied historically.) It follows from the analysis of representativeness offered earlier, of course, that there are severe limits to the action any individual voter can take if the MP is not representing his or her opinions. Interestingly, although Parliamentary votes are always recorded, the news media only publicize the names of MPs for and against motions in unusual circumstances: first, when there are rebels abstaining or voting against the party whip, and secondly when there is a 'free' vote. At the time of writing, the last complete list of names for and against a motion published in the serious national press concerned a vote on the continued rejection of capital punishment. The vote on capital punishment has been a free vote because it has been thought to raise questions of morality which should be above party politics, but there is no doubt in the evidence from opinion polls that were a referendum to be held on the matter the electorate would take a different view from the House of Commons. This perception prompted the following leading article in the London *Daily Mail*.

MPS SNUB THE ELECTORS

THE Commons vote went heavily against those who want capital punishment restored. In so doing members defied public opinion which has consistently and strongly favoured restoration ever since its abolition in 1965.

This gap in attitudes is worrying. It suggests that MPs are seriously out of touch. Their lives are of course more sheltered than those of their constituents. The Commons may be less decorous than it was, but, even so, its members lack the experience of erupting violence of those outside its walls. The rising tide of savagery doesn't disturb them as it does the voters who are at the receiving end. It is all very well for those, like Roy Hattersley in Tuesday's debate, who condemn the primitive popular desire for retribution, but that desire is almost universal. The great mass of people want to hit back at the criminals. They seek revenge – which Bacon called 'a wild kind of justice'. They want to give criminals some of their own medicine and it is no good telling them that such urges are uncivilised.

This gulf between the opinion of the lawmakers and that of the people is dangerous because it tends to bring the law into popular contempt. In extreme circumstances it may lead to the nightmare of people taking the law into their own hands, with such consequences as we see in Ulster.

It must however be said of the debate that it did justice to the gravity of the subject. Home Secretary Douglas Hurd in particular made some telling points. In the end, the members voted according to their consciences and with their consciences they will henceforth have to live.

We may note in passing that this free vote produced not a single Labour member supporting the amendment. The so-called workers' party could not find one member to share the overwhelming working class belief that the death penalty should be revived.

We are now unlikely to see the law on capital punishment changed in this parliament. Thus the priority must be to ensure that long sentences for murder are not made a mockery of in practice and that 'life' really does mean 'life'. That way, at least, some of the people's anger at their rulers' inadequacy in dealing with the present wave of violence may be assuaged.

Daily Mail

The point is simply that openness is a necessary condition of accountability, but not sufficient to enforce either accountability or representativeness.

Of course, just because a voting system is being employed is no reason to assume that accountability of those casting a vote is desirable. But it may be important to separate questions of limited accountability from questions of general publicity. Arguments for accountability could easily be outweighed by countervailing considerations about other consequences of publicity. For example, imagine a jury which returned a majority vote convicting someone of violent crime. There might be a case for accountability here, since declaring a verdict is an important exercise of public power. Nevertheless, it is easy to find overriding considerations against publicity. It would be against the public interest for the names of jurors voting 'guilty' to be known, first because of the risk to their personal safety, secondly because jurors who were held accountable for their individual verdicts would fear being hounded whatever verdict they returned, and thirdly, given those two reasons, because it would become much harder to find willing and honest jurors. But while all this suggests that it would be undesirable for jurors' votes to be published in newspapers, we could still insist that jurors be accountable in a more limited sense: they should account to one another for the verdict they wish to return. They should be accountable to one another but not to 'outsiders'. A jury deciding on the single issue of the guilt of the accused is like a direct democracy, and all the points made earlier apply to it. When unanimity is required, the need for mutual accountability is enhanced by the power of veto which each juror possesses.

The question of the accountability of the voter in a system of representative government might usefully be explored by considering a comparison between the MP, the juror, and the citizen. The MPs' votes should be public knowledge to provide a 'feedback' mechanism; they will have to take account of the reactions of those who will come to have this information when they vote. This may well mean that, on occasion, MPs will be pulled in different directions by the expected reactions of their parties and their constituents, or by either or both of those and their consciences. But it does mean that they cannot simply ignore the electors as would be possible under a secret vote. Accountability is supposed to ensure that the electors do not lose every vestige of control over MPs, so the publicity is to restrict power.

This same restriction gives point to the secrecy of a jury's deliberations: it helps to protect individuals from interference from powerful groups – whether these be friends of the accused, the police, and so on. The danger of bribery and intimidation is, of course, the standard argument for the secret ballot, which we shall consider below. Here we may remark that the absence of the individual accountability of jurors is designed to eliminate the undesirable influence of outsiders, just as publicity in the MP's case is designed to ensure that the desirable influence of electoral opinion is not excluded.

Is the citizen casting a vote in an election to be protected from outsiders, like the jury, or exposed to their scrutiny, like the MP? As we saw earlier, John Stuart Mill favoured exposure, because voting was a public act for which the voter was answerable to others. But it is important to note that his argument for accountability is not that the voter should be influenced by others; rather, the individual voter should be open to the persuasion of those with superior arguments, that only certain sorts of argument (about the public interest) should enter into the discussion, and that to be answerable was to be made aware that the voter owed a duty to the rest of the community to cast a ballot in a conscientious attempt to promote the public interest.

It might seem as if this is an argument to the conclusion that voters should be willing to defend their voting intentions rather than to the conclusion that they should be willing to defend the way in which they cast their vote. Might not these arguments be met by a convention that, rather than avoid 'politics' as a subject for discussion, we should encourage it? If the point is to expose the voter to a variety of arguments about which candidate is best able to look after the public interest, then that may be achieved by open discussion before the election, without requiring an open ballot. This brings out the fact that Mill's argument runs together two notions which we may want to separate: first, the openness of the voter to persuasion; secondly, the accountability of the voter for the discharge of a public duty. The first requirement can be met by open discussion, but the second requires an open ballot. The reason, of course, is that in the absence of an open ballot there can be no check that the voter, apparently convinced that the public interest requires the election of X, and apparently therefore intending to vote for X, does not in the event vote for Y in the pursuit of narrow self-interest. Mill was mainly concerned to avoid this last result, of self-interested voting.

Commitment

This brings us to the notion of commitment as a second reason for openness in the ballot. Again, the comparison between the MP, the voter and the juror brings out the points to be made. If an MP is associated with a particular legislative intention, or public policy position, either through Parliamentary activity, or, more usually, through activities inside and outside Parliament, he or she is committed to voting in particular ways within Parliament. But the MP may well suffer the same pull between the requirements of the pursuit of the public interest and the requirements of self-interest. It would be hazardous, therefore, to allow MPs to vote secretly: at the extreme, we might find all of them supporting policy A in debate, but an alternative being adopted in a secret ballot. Similarly, jurors need to be accountable to each other, if not to the rest of the community (see above). An open discussion about the defendant's guilt, followed by a secret ballot on it, would at best be very inefficient, since no-one would know who remained to be convinced, and at worst encourage corruption. In both cases, openness is partly a requirement about defending the way a vote has been cast, the backward-looking notion of accountability, but it is also a requirement about consistency, the forward-looking notion of commitment. Mill's argument stresses the first, but his concerns with open debate and persuasion go further to embrace the second.

We may bring in considerations drawn from Rousseau's democratic theory at this point. If Mill's case for openness is that it encourages public-spirited voting, while secrecy encourages self-interested voting, Rousseau's requirement that the general will should come from all and apply to all in acts of sovereignty similarly contrasts the public orientation of the general will and the selfish orientation of the wills aggregated into the will of all. Obviously, open voting would not be sufficient to ensure that voters do not vote selfishly, but the combination of open debate and open voting is designed to encourage public spiritedness. One interpretation of Rousseau's idea that citizens could be 'forced to be free' is that freedom consists in following the dictates of the (morally inspired) general will, rather than the desires of (morally inferior) self-interest.[5] Open voting, and indeed compulsory voting, might be expected to encourage this freedom, although it could not guarantee it.

The discussion so far has related open voting to a particular sort of commitment: a commitment that a voter's intentions (the reasons and arguments he or she gives, that the public interest requires a certain course of action) should be carried through in the way that the vote is actually cast. In so far as both Mill and Rousseau took the ballot to be an expression of the public interest, the particular danger for them was that secrecy would encourage self-interestedness in voting. But the idea of 'commitment' has a wider relevance in voting systems, which has been articulated by trade unions' defence of open balloting at the place of work. It is time to consider these arguments, and consider if they are relevant to electoral voting.

The Conservative government's industrial legislation has included the 'reform' of trade union procedures when industrial action, the partial or complete withdrawal of labour, is contemplated. The legislation requires that there be a ballot of the membership. The absence of a proper ballot affects the legal immunities of the trade unions and exposes them to injunctions about the industrial action. The case for the secret ballot (which may take place at the workplace, or be postal) largely concerned alleged intimidation.[6] While an open ballot exposed individuals to unfair and undesirable pressure from others in the workforce, it was said, a secret ballot protected them and enabled them to state their 'true' opinion on the desirability of the proposed industrial action. This anti-intimidation argument, of course, applies directly to electoral systems, and will be expanded below.

Many trades unions, for example the National Union of Railwaymen, opposed this legislative interference with the traditional practice of open voting at the workplace. One of the reasons was the argument we have considered above: to vote on strike action is a public act, because it involves the future of the group as a whole, and therefore accountability. A second argument, the one we want to consider in more detail here, concerns commitment. Strike action is costly, but its chances of success are directly related to the number of persons pursuing it.

There is, of course, a classic collective action (or Olson) problem here, of the kind we described in Chapter 2.[7] The claims of solidarity may run counter to self-interest narrowly conceived. The union's worry concerned the commitment to strike action expressed in a vote for it. If I vote openly for strike action, I commit myself to it: others will know I have done so and will be able to remind me of my decision when I am tempted back to work by the costs of striking. Because of this public commitment, I directly involve myself in the action taken by all.

There is obviously a difference between this notion of commitment, and the one considered previously. In the first case, the commitment is to vote in a certain way, given the reasons one holds. In this second case, the commitment is to take the action for which one has voted. The danger of the secret ballot, from the union's point of view, is that individual secret voting does not carry the same psychological force. I may put a cross on a ballot paper in the privacy of my own home, and post it off for counting. I will feel, it is alleged, that I am voting for what the union should do, without the commitment to do it myself. Clearly, this 'psychological' point is open to empirical dispute. But if we assume it is correct, does it have any relevance for electoral systems rather than directly democratic procedures?

The point certainly applies to MPs themselves. When they vote on legislation, they are choosing a course of action for the whole community. When James Mill considered mechanisms designed to align the interests of individual voters with those of their representatives, he suggested that short Parliaments would be an advantage. Such Parliaments would ensure, he thought, not only that representatives were regularly subject to the sanction of loss of office, but also that MPs would be less inclined to separate their position as representatives from their role as citizens (Lively and Rees 1978). The policies they supported as MPs would therefore be those they could support as citizens. In a way, this is akin to the arguments we have already reviewed: it links to Rousseau's concern with the general will, and with John Stuart Mill's arguments against secrecy at the ballot box. But whereas Rousseau was discussing citizen-legislators, and Mill was discussing voters choosing a representative, James Mill was focusing on the role of the representative. Again, we have already seen that open voting by MPs is an essential requirement of accountability, and that open voting is favoured by trades unions concerned that the act of voting should carry commitment. James Mill's argument combines the points when applied to voting by representatives.

Nevertheless, this does not show that the argument about

commitment applies to electors, rather than to those who are making policy decisions. The relevant argument in the electors' case is usually expressed rather differently: that voting expresses some commitment to outcomes. We should consider what these 'outcomes' might be, and how the open or secret character of voting might affect the issue.

We saw in Chapter 4 that the doctrine of a mandate holds that the winners of an election are entitled to carry into effect (at least) the policies they proposed to the electorate. On this view, the elector's decision to cast a vote in favour of a particular party platform expresses a preference for that package of policies over any other package, and legitimizes its implementation. The elector is taken to be committed to those policies, in the sense that he or she is not entitled to complain when they are carried out. The openness or secrecy of the ballot is not particularly relevant, except in the sense that the ballot should be arranged so that the elector expresses his or her true preferences.

We expressed considerable reservations about the adequacy of this argument in the present conditions of British political practice. These reservations surround the plurality system and the packaging of policies in manifestos. But there is another way in which mandating is theoretically relevant even though it is not pursued in British Parliamentary practice. One relationship between a constituency and a representative body is created by delegation. In this model, the persons represented determine how their delegate should vote at the representative body. In effect, they decide amongst themselves on the favoured policies, and the elected delegate is required to vote in particular ways as a result. This system embodies a far stronger notion of the delegate's mandate. Because the voters are discussing policies, the argument about commitment in relation to open voting is relevant, even though the final policy decision will be taken by a representative body. For example, trades unions often take decisions about industrial action this way. Local organizations discuss the policy, make a decision, and choose one of their number to attend a general meeting and cast a vote accordingly.[8] In the context of national politics, a decision about declaring war, for example, might make the notion of commitment, and its connection with open voting, highly relevant.

When the 'outcome' is not interpreted under the manifesto–mandate doctrine, it is associated instead with the idea that participation legitimizes the system by which decisions are taken. Here again, openness or secrecy is not the primary issue. But it is nevertheless important, if the argument is to have any validity, that the method by which votes are cast does enable some expression of true preferences about what is taken to be legitimized. The extent to which these true preferences can be expressed depends on other aspects of the voting system which will be discussed in this and the next chapter. The dispute as to whether secret or open voting is to be preferred is largely (but not wholly) about which system is more likely to allow for the true preferences to be stated. We can consider this again when we have looked at the case for the secret ballot. Finally, we should recall the importance of commitment in the analysis of strategic voting, logrolling and vote trading. Here the relevant aspect of commitment is in relation to trust and predictability. Those who dislike logrolling and strategic voting claim that the voter's expressed preferences are not his or her true ones, reproducing the central question about openness and secrecy.

ARGUMENTS FOR SECRECY

When secret voting to elect MPs was introduced the primary argument was that the extension of the franchise was to no avail without the secret ballot, because of the dangers of intimidation.[9] Intimidation here refers to threats associated with superior economic power. In a society of great economic inequality, in which the poor depended on the rich for work and housing, open voting made the former vulnerable. The economic consequences of their not voting as they were expected to were so serious that they made a mockery of the freedom to vote. It is important to remember the local base of class power. Local magnates who had effectively been able to control who was elected relied both on the limited franchise and on their economic power. Radicals who argued for the extension of the franchise were clear that it would be useless unless accompanied by the secret ballot. No-one is likely nowadays to deny that this was a compelling argument in the nineteenth century and beyond. But we might ask how we should interpret the idea of intimidation, and whether contemporary economic inequalities present the same dangers.

Thinking about 'intimidation' forces us to refine the idea of 'true preferences' which was employed earlier. The dispute between supporters and opponents of secret voting, in different contexts, concerns the voter's ability to cast a vote for what he or she really prefers.[10] The same question arises in the dispute as to whether strategic voting and logrolling are anti-democratic practices to be condemned, or extensions of democracy to be welcomed. Both disputes raise a problem about how we should interpret 'real preferences'.

Let us take an example of intimidation. In an election in which ballots are not cast secretly, A tells B that B will lose his job, and the cottage to which it entitles him, unless B votes for candidate C. C favours policies supportive of the interests of A; B would vote for another candidate D

without this intervention by A. This is undoubtedly a case of intimidation of the kind that a secret ballot makes less probable. A secret ballot also makes bribery less appealing, because A could not then know how B voted and might waste his or her money. So the secret ballot is designed to render both threats and offers to the voter unattractive, leaving the voter free to express his or her 'real' preference, that is the preference in the absence of that threatening or offering intervention. If we assume that the threat or offer is successful, then its effect is to change the preference expressed. But it is misleading to say that the new preference is not the voter's 'real' preference. It is his or her first preference *in the new situation*.

This is exactly parallel to the situation in strategic voting and logrolling. A voter A who would like candidate C to win, but chooses to vote for D in the belief that only D has a chance to defeat E, might appear not to be expressing his or her 'real' preference. But this new preference for D is real enough: this new preference differs from the old because it takes account of the likely votes of others, and in that sense is based on more information than the old preference. So the parallel between the intimidation example and the strategic voting example is that there is a change of preference in both cases, and that in both cases the new preference is genuinely most preferred given the new situation.

The difference in the two examples, of course, is that the new situation is deliberately created by outside intervention in the case of intimidation, but is created by the voter's own calculation of advantage in the case of strategic voting. The objection to threats and inducements made to the voter is not that the voter's preferences cease to be real, but that they are based on considerations that ought to be excluded from his or her voting decision. The strategic voter takes account of others' preferences; the intimidated (or bribed) voter makes someone else's preferences his or her own. Strategic voting does not undermine political equality in the way that successful threats and bribes do. We might note that party platforms, too, can be interpreted as threats and offers,[11] but while intimidation works directly on the self-interest of the voter, such threats and offers may refer to the voter's non-selfish concerns. Nevertheless, promises of tax breaks for particular sections of the community are still described as electoral bribes.

To what extent are such threats and bribes a danger today, if elections were not secret? Clearly, there is still great economic inequality in society, and the temptation to exploit economic advantage remains. To some extent it is moderated by the size of constituencies, but we should remember that the gains from intervention are dependent on the number of votes which need to be changed by corrupt practices, not by the size of the total electorate. In any case, even a secret ballot is no protection against voters being induced to stay away from the polls. But the privacy of voting is defended not only in the face of economic inequality, but also in the face of other pressures. One is physical force (for example, in Northern Ireland and certain African states). Another comes from within the family. People who live together do not necessarily have the same politics, and many couples vote for different parties. A secret ballot isolates each voter from this consideration.

CONCLUSION

The contrast between the contemporary notion that voting is a private act, and John Stuart Mill's idea that it was a public duty is thus clear. The secret ballot is supposed to make the voter independent of influences thought undesirable, and able to express preferences sanitized from outside pressure; the open ballot, for Mill, reinforced the independent spirit of the voter by exposing him or her to the need to defend how it was used. Underlying both views is a deeper view of the considerations which an elector ought to take into account, and those he or she ought to leave aside.

Mill's argument was strengthened, as he pointed out, when the suffrage was limited. Those who chose the decision-makers should account to those who were not entitled to do so for their action. Clearly, universal suffrage weakens this. The secret ballot was a necessary accompaniment of the extension of the franchise, and of democracy conceived as political equality. The consequence may well be as Mill predicted: that the voter thinks of the vote as a right, not a duty, and is encouraged to consider his or her self-interest rather than the general good when casting it. If the secrecy of voting in Parliamentary elections remains desirable taking account of conflicting considerations, we should not assume that secret ballots are always superior in all situations in which votes are cast.

This chapter has concentrated on an important component of ballot structure, the secret ballot, which has been unduly neglected in much modern discussion. Our next chapter takes up questions arising from another 'phase' in Rae's typology – constituency structure. Because of the particular history of British electoral practice, discussed in Chapter 3, our consideration of constituency structure will form part of a wider treatment of the territorial dimensions of British elections.

6 The territorial dimension of elections

INTRODUCTION

Constituency structure

One of the most important ways in which systems for electing representatives may differ relates to what, in Chapter 3, we called 'constituency structure'. Perhaps the most fundamental distinction to be drawn in connection with this concerns whether an entire electorate votes in the same electoral unit or whether the voters are divided up into separate 'units'. To illuminate the point consider the difference between the French and American presidential elections. In French presidential elections there is one national constituency – voters in Marseille who voted for François Mitterand in the 1988 election had their vote added to those of all other voters for Mitterrand, whether those voters lived in Paris, Rennes or anywhere else in France. But in the United States voters in each state elect a delegation to the Electoral College, and it is then the members of this College who choose the President. Consequently someone in New York who voted for George Bush in 1988 would not have had their vote added to that of a Bush voter in California; it was added only to the votes cast for Bush in the state of New York. Because in the United States smaller 'units', in this case the states, come between the voter and the election result, it is possible that the winning candidate may receive fewer votes from the mass electorate than the defeated opponent. Indeed, this has happened in US presidential elections – the election of 1888 being the most recent undisputed instance.[1]

The argument for dividing up voters into smaller 'units' in presidential elections usually rests on the claim that these 'units' are significant foci of identity for the voters, and that the legitimacy of an election result might be cast in doubt if the successful candidate merely had to win a plurality among the voters. However, the case for dividing electorates into smaller 'units' becomes more complex when many representatives have to be selected, and it is, of course, this situation which confronts Parliamentary systems, such as Britain's.

Before turning to examine the advantages and disadvantages of sub-dividing electorates in this way, we must first remember an obvious, though sometimes forgotten, point. While the sub-division of electorate into territorial units is often the basis on which 'units' of voters are created, it is not the only possible basis of division. Some form of functional representation might be practised – either as an alternative or a complement to territorial representation. For instance, a sports club which provides facilities for several different sports might have an executive committee composed of representatives of the players of each of the sports, with the representatives elected by their fellow players. In terms of ensuring that the most important interests in the club are represented adequately, it would probably make more sense for this club than creating territorially defined constituencies. It is possible, of course, that club members who live in different places may also have conflicting interests, and thus justify elections on a territorial basis too, but it is more likely that conflict of interest would emerge between the different sports.

Functional representation

Some political theorists, most notably the early twentieth-century English pluralist G.D.H. Cole (1920), have advocated functional representation at the level of the state.[2] Indeed, it can be argued that some functional representation is actually practised in modern Britain through a system of 'corporatist' interest representation involving economic groups (Dearlove and Saunders 1984: 422–3). But in the modern state it would be very difficult, and arguably impossible, to establish some form of fair functional representation in an elected assembly. The problem lies in knowing how many seats to allocate to each of the interests that might claim representation. Even in a club this could be problematic – for example, the football players might claim that they should have more representatives because they regularly field more teams than the hockey players, while the latter might claim greater representation, because they have more players 'on the books' even though many of them play only irregularly.

John Stuart Mill thought that the representation of non-territorial interests could be effected by the introduction of the kind of electoral system proposed by Thomas Hare in the mid nineteenth century. Mill's support for Hare's system was based on its allowing voters to register support for someone who was not a candidate in their own locality. He was particularly afraid of class voting because of geographical concentrations of social classes. Mill (1910: 264) believed that Hare's scheme benefited minorities who 'would look out elsewhere for a candidate likely to obtain other votes in addition to their own'. Of course, Mill himself did not want voters to vote according to their economic interests, but might not Hare's system facilitate economic interests to mobilize and elect their own representatives? The answer to this question is probably yes, but there are two reasons for not attaching much significance to it. First, the presence of political parties, of which Mill took no account, under such arrangements would mean that the role of the economic interests in the national political system would probably be little different from their current role. Secondly, even in the absence of parties, Mill's argument about the ability of minorities to gain political representation does not allow for the fact that some kinds of minorities have access to vast political resources while others do not. For example, British farmers have been able to mobilize far more resources than either pensioners or consumers. In general, well-organized minorities are more able to motivate their members to cast their vote appropriately in constituencies where such votes would be effective in electing a supportive candidate. Consequently, we must conclude that this mechanism does not provide a means of effecting a direct form of fair functional representation.

The advantage of territorial sub-divisions is that problems of defining the relevant sub-units are easier than for functional representation, although we shall see that this matter is still far from being uncontroversial. But, if most Parliamentary systems provide for territorially based representation from sub-units, not all of them do so. In Iceland, for example, there is a single national constituency, so that there, as in French presidential elections, the vote of each elector has a direct impact on every other voter. (Especially in the United States, an election in a single constituency like this is referred to as an 'at-large' election.) The British practice, of organizing electoral contests in territorial sub-units, is thus not essential in providing for citizen representation in a nation state.

We have already seen (in Chapter 3) how territorial representation developed in Britain. In this chapter we are concerned with three rather different questions. (1) In terms of the representation of citizens, what, in general, are the relative advantages and disadvantages of organizing elections in territorial sub-units? (2) In what ways is the potential conflict between the representation of people and the representation of places resolved in Britain? (3) And what are the consequences for the British political system of having Parliamentary elections based on territorially defined single-member constituencies?

THE ADVANTAGES AND DISADVANTAGES OF TERRITORIAL SUB-UNITS

When examining the merits of using territorial sub-units in electing representatives it is important to separate, at least initially, this issue from the debate over how to aggregate votes. A system employing a proportional formula to aggregate votes might be based on a single national constituency (as in Iceland), or on territorial sub-units (as in Ireland), or on some combination of the two principles (as in West Germany). Equally a plurality system can be used to aggregate votes in either a single national constituency or in territorial sub-units of the whole. In fact, among those nation states which employ plurality voting, the former system is not used – largely because in any body in which there are organized parties or factions plurality voting in an at-large election would often lead to the non-representation of opposition groups. Very often the winners would literally take all. Since, for a variety of reasons, some voice for representatives of the defeated in a legislative assembly is usually thought to be desirable, plurality voting at the level of the state is invariably used in conjunction with geographically defined sub-constituencies.[3] (As we shall later, though, this analytic separation of constituency structure from electoral formulae cannot be sustained completely.) In this section we shall examine the following question: are there any good reasons favouring an exclusively territorial system of representation?

One of the principal arguments used to justify territorially–based sub-units in an electoral system is that the representative can have much greater contact with those people he or she represents. If there was an at-large election for the House of Commons, each MP would be representing 40,000,000 potential voters; but by placing the 650 MPs in single-member constituencies, the electorate to which each of them is accountable is (typically) about 60,000 strong. As it stands, this argument for sub-dividing the electorate is not very convincing – at least not in the case of the larger nation states, such as Britain. Even the most conscientious legislator could retain personal contact with only a relatively small proportion of the total number of people he or she represents. Most people could expect to have no opportunity to express their views, or outline their problems, to such a representative. In this regard the citizen is little better off in an electorate of 60,000 than in one of 40,000,000. Of course, this argument about retaining contact is not entirely specious: representation by territorial sub-units does make a difference when the sub-units can be made sufficiently small that the representative can know all those represented on a personal basis. The problem lies in the fact that there is an upper limit to the size a representative body can be without loss of effectiveness as a deliberating institution. The House of Commons is one of the largest legislative chambers among the liberal democracies, and is already close to this limit.

Even if there were an at-large election, the system could still permit individual MPs to retain contact with a particular territorial unit. For instance, this would be easily operable where there were organized parties: each party might simply allocate to each of its MPs a particular geographical area for which they would have special responsibility, in much the same way that ministerial and shadow-ministerial portfolios are distributed. The point is, then, that, if the argument for territorial constituencies were to rest only on the possibility of greater contact between representative and represented, it would be unconvincing in societies of more than a few hundred thousand people.

Consequently, those who support territorially–based sub-units for a system of representation usually rest their case on a rather different argument. This is the claim that the people represented will have important interests which will vary from one locale to another; in the absence of territorial representation, not all of these interests are likely to be well represented. This argument has some force – even for societies where there are many important interests which are not geographically based. The precise site for a projected new airport, the location of a nuclear power plant, and the awarding of government contracts to particular firms are all instances of decisions which distribute benefits unevenly between geographical areas. While everyone may benefit in some respects from a new airport, those whom it is built close to suffer from the noise of aircraft, and will have an interest in getting it located elsewhere. The larger the constituency, the more particular territorial interests are likely to be ignored, and this problem is manifested most in a single national constituency. No society can ever get away from the fundamental fact that people must occupy physical space, and because of this the interests of people in one geographical area may well come to conflict with those in another.

But what follows from this? Clearly, it suggests that in many institutions, and certainly in the state itself, there is a strong case for having some form of territorially–based representation. Parties merely allocating their MPs to be 'responsible' for particular geographical areas would yield insufficient protection for territorial interests. But there are two reasons for rejecting the claim that this constitutes a case for having an exclusively territorial system of representation. First, purely territorial representation is likely to exacerbate differences between different areas, and make it more difficult for common interests to be weighed adequately in relation to particular geographical ones. This is evident in the United States, where relatively weak political parties allow for local self-interest to have a disproportionate influence in the making of public policy. Secondly, there may be other important interests which divide different groups in a society, but which do not have a territorial basis, and which may find it more difficult to get on to the political agenda if representation in the state is solely territorial in nature. That groups may enjoy functional representation outside the electoral process, through a corporatist framework, should not be overlooked, but it is only certain kinds of economic interests that usually gain access to the state in this way.

Nevertheless, while introducing functional representation into the argument does not help the case for an exclusive territorial basis for electoral representation, it does provide a case for there being some form of territorial electoral representation. The power of those groups which are part of a corporatist system may mean that it is only through organizations formed around territorial representation that any opposition can be mobilized. As Dearlove and Saunders (1984: 423) point out:

> The bargains and compromises which are reached at central level as a result of closed negotiations between state agencies and corporate interests today increasingly come under challenge from below (most notably through radical local councils and nationalist movements at the periphery) as a result of the mobilisation of non-incorporated interests through territorial strategies and alliances. Functional and territorial organization constantly clash precisely because territory remains important as the basis for opposition to centrally determined policy-making.

Because of the ease with which certain interests gain access to government through a neo-corporatist system, it is important to retain structures around which potential opposition can mobilize. Local party organizations, centred on territorially-defined Parliamentary constituencies, constitute one of these structures. Without them, the biases in a representative system of a liberal–capitalist state are likely to increase.

Finally, in considering the advantages of the geographical sub-division of elections, two spurious claims must be rejected. One is the contention that the powerful benefit from large electoral units, and that new interests can best organize themselves initially in smaller constituencies. On this view small electoral districts make it easier for the representatives of new interests to get elected – small is beautiful. It is true, of course, that more resources are required to fight a national election than a local one, and that small parties may not be able to acquire the minimum amount necessary to mount an effective contest. But unless such a party has a high level of support in a particular locale, it cannot make an electoral breakthrough at the local level either.[4] Indeed, the main barrier facing such parties is not the size of the total electorate they must mobilize but the threshhold, in terms of voter support, they must cross in plurality voting systems in order to elect representatives at any level. Furthermore, powerful interests can make their resources count far more in local election contests than they can in the 'set battles' of national contests.

The other spurious claim is that locally based elections will stimulate voter participation more than purely national elections. There is no evidence for this whatsoever, and indeed the opposite seems to be the case. For example, in virtually all liberal democracies voter turnout is far lower in local elections of various sorts, and the countries which have purely national elections do not have lower turnouts than similar countries in which at least some Parliamentary seats are contested on a territorial basis.[5]

However, in addition to the points made earlier, there are two major objections to territorial sub-units as the basis of representation. The first is that in any election in which a constituency is sub-divided it becomes difficult to ensure that, overall, the result parallels the result that would have been produced by an at-large election. People may be distributed geographically in such a way that it becomes virtually impossible for constituency boundaries to be drawn so that there is an exact correspondence between the distribution of the total vote and the representatives actually elected. This problem is usually made much worse by the use of plurality voting, and other non-proportional formulae, but it can still be evident in electoral systems which employ proportional formulae to aggregate votes.[6] Of course, in some representative institutions the idea that it is *people* which are being represented either is not accepted at all or is only one principle informing the representative system. For example, in the US Senate it is the *states* which are represented, and until 1913 the Constitution specified that Senators were to be chosen by their respective state legislatures. Even though they are now popularly elected, no-one ever questions whether the results of Senate elections reflect the national pattern of the distribution of votes between the parties. And, as we saw in Chapter 3, in Britain the idea that people should be represented in Parliament was grafted on to the earlier notion of the representation of geographically defined interests. It is not surprising, then, that today there is still a conflict in the organization of elections to the House of Commons between the principle that people should be represented and the principle that it is places which are being represented.

The second objection to the use of territorial sub-units is that, unlike a single national constituency, the composition of these sub-units is open to manipulation. Of course, there are many other ways in which electoral rules can be manipulated by interested actors – as was the case with franchise extension in nineteenth-century Britain, when the issue of who could be excluded from the franchise was a central factor in making the qualifications for the vote very complex. But today the definition of constituency boundaries is one of the most powerful instruments available to enable a party to retain office. It was used in this way in recent years by the former governing party in Queensland, and the practice has a long history in the United States.

On balance, however, the argument for some form of territorial representation in a state seems strong – indeed, the case for this form of representation is probably stronger for the state itself than for many organizations within the state. Most especially it can serve as a partial check against the biases of the indirect functional representation of major economic interests. Yet at the same time there are several respects in which territorial representation makes it more difficult for a system of fair representation of all affected interests to be sustained. This suggests that a democrat is likely to advocate a system of limited territorial representation – for example, one combining it with national (at-large) elections. Nevertheless, while so far we have succeeded in discussing the question of constituency structure without becoming enmeshed in the debate about electoral formulae, it is now important to recognize that in the British context the two issues are intertwined. This point is best made by outlining one of the best-known popular arguments about the British electoral system. It proceeds as follows.

The representation of people involves more than just representing their views. In an election people can only express a preference for one candidate – they cannot choose *how* they want to be governed. In particular, they cannot choose whether they want to be governed by a single party with an overall Parliamentary majority or by a coalition of parties. While it is true that the British electoral system does not reflect in Parliament the levels of support for all parties in the country, and in particular it usually exaggerates greatly the support for the winning party, this system does allow for the formation of stable, majority governments. Because this provides for continuity and consistency in the policy-making process, the interests of the people are better represented than they would be by a system that better reflected levels of party support among voters. While it is plurality voting which provides for single-party rule, territorial representation is an integral part of this stable system of government, since it ensures that at least some other interests can be represented in Parliament. Without territorial representation the regime would probably be much less stable, because all opposition would likely have to be conducted on an extra-Parliamentary basis.

Of course, one of the main premises of this argument – that the only alternative to single-party rule based on plurality voting is a French Fourth Republic model of short-lived, unstable governments with no clear policy programmes – is nonsense. Stable coalition governments with clear policy programmes exist in many countries which utilize proportional formulae for aggregating the vote. But quite how British parties would respond faced by the need to bargain with potential coalition partners in government is a matter on which there is likely to be disagreement; it might be that a system of unstable coalition governments would emerge and thereby British voters would not have their interests represented well. If so, then there would be a case for linking the quality of representation to its territorial character. This is because the argument outlined above is correct in asserting that to abandon the exclusively territorial basis of elections in Britain would entail either an implicit commitment to adopt some form of proportional representation in allocating Parliamentary seats, or the acceptance of even more lopsided majorities in Parliament. The case for long-lived and stable, if 'unrepresentative', governments based on plurality voting is intimately connected, then, with territorial representation. But how, in Britain, are the claims of 'territory' and of 'people' to be reconciled?

BRITAIN: REPRESENTING PERSONS AND PLACES

We saw in Chapter 3 that in the nineteenth century disputes about the reapportionment of Parliamentary seats lay at the heart of much of the debate about Parliamentary reform. It was not until 1944 that legislation to create a permanent Boundary Commission was enacted. In one respect this legislation can be seen as recognition that, in the absence of a single national constituency, there is indeed a significant territorial dimension to establishing democracy at the level of the state. But the

British way of dealing with this dimension, which involves de-politicizing it, is not the only approach, and it is useful to contrast it with the American experience, which is of a far more politicized process of 'territorial electoral management'. Indeed, it is perhaps useful to begin with the United States because it illuminates just how much can be at stake in controlling the division of territory for electoral purposes.

Along with Captain C.C. Boycott and a few other individuals in the English-speaking world, Mr Elbridge Gerry has achieved lasting fame through his surname being used to create an eponym in the English language. It was for an action as Governor of Massachusetts in 1812 that Gerry is usually remembered – he created a salamander-shaped congressional district to give an advantage to his own political party in subsequent congressional elections. From this action was created the word 'gerrymander' – the arranging of electoral districts in such a way that one party can elect more representatives than it could under a fair system of electoral districting. (It was a cartoonist who had pointed out that the shape of the Massachusetts district resembled that of a salamander.) In nineteenth-century America many aspects of the system of political representation were highly politicized – virtually all federal government jobs were political appointments, so that there was nothing unusual in placing the drawing of electoral boundaries in the hands of politicians. But although political reform at the beginning of this century resulted in many areas of administration being removed from direct political influence, political control of the representative system itself remained. The Supreme Court, which might have intervened to stop the unfair drawing of electoral boundaries, chose not to do so for many years – deeming the issue to be essentially political in nature and hence outside its brief. In practice this meant that rural interests were often greatly overrepresented in Congress and in state legislatures at the expense of urban interests. It was not until 1962 that, in a series of cases, the Court reversed its approach, and required states to construct electoral boundaries for legislatures that were as close in size (in terms of those eligible to vote) as possible.

The Supreme Court was concerned with one question only – was the 'weight' of a voter in one territorial unit the same as that in any other territorial unit? At first this approach took no account of the idea that places should be represented – electoral districts had to be mathematically equal in size even if this meant adding on part of a city to a district which consisted mainly of another city which was miles away. Subsequently, however, the Court amended the principle of voter equality to allow constituency sizes to vary by up to 15 per cent. However, these decisions did nothing to require that electoral districts be as compact as possible, and, indeed, there are two reasons why salamander-shaped districts are still very much a part of the American political scene. First, other Supreme Court decisions in the 1960s relating to civil rights require that electoral boundaries be drawn in such a way as to permit the fair representation of racial minorities. This requirement can result in some very 'un-compact' districts; for example, the Seventeenth Congressional District in New York has a voting age population of 442,000 but in places it is no wider than one block of apartment buildings. Secondly, the Supreme Court has not touched on the issue of whether electoral boundaries may be drawn in such a way as to advantage one party over the other. That practice is still perfectly legal, so that, where possible, politicians try to draw electoral boundaries to maximize the number of seats their party will win; sometimes, as in the Democrat-controlled redistricting in California in 1981, they succeed in doing so by their creativity in constructing oddly shaped districts.

It is because politicians still control the redistricting process in states like California that gerrymandering can still occur – and, in fact, it has become more 'scientific' in execution. Even in states where the drawing of electoral boundaries is supposedly in the hands of independent commissions, these are often open to political manipulation in terms of the officials appointed or elected to such commissions.

In contrast to this, the British approach, as informed by the 1944 legislation, has been to place responsibility for the construction of Parliamentary districts in the hands of independent Boundary Commissioners. There is one Commission each for England, Scotland, Wales and Northern Ireland; for each Commission there are three nominated Commissioners, who are joined by two assessors and the Speaker of the House of Commons (Johnston 1983: 13). One important point about the Commission is that its members have not been political appointees, and the only party input to the process of drawing up Parliamentary boundaries comes from the right to submit evidence once the Commission has put forward draft proposals and in debate when the proposals are sent to Parliament. But, equally significant, is that, despite the many contrasts with the explicitly political American approach, no effort is made in Britain either to ensure that the results, in terms of seats won by the parties, reflect as much as possible the distribution of the vote. The brief of the Commission is to construct boundaries that are as close in size as is practicable, and not to provide a way in which votes can be linked to seats.

There are several ways in which territory further impinges on the fair representation of all voters in Britain. One cause of this is the special treatment accorded to Scotland, Wales and Northern Ireland, because of their distinctive history. As we noted in Chapter 3, an operating principle of the Commission has been that the seats in Scotland and Wales (presently seventy two and thirty eight respectively) may not be reduced in number – because this would stir up nationalistic resentment. Since the Commons is already a large legislature, there has been a tendency at each electoral reapportionment to increase its size just enough to remove the worst anomalies. Even so in the 1980s the typical English constituency has about 25 per cent more people eligible to vote in it than its Scottish counterpart. Until 1978 Northern Ireland was deliberately under-represented at Westminster, on the grounds that it had control over many of its own affairs through the Stormont Parliament. However, the imposition of direct rule in 1972 made this situation anomalous, and the loss of the Labour government's majority in 1977 enabled the province's MPs to exert pressure for a 50 per cent increase in its Parliamentary representation. Today Northern Ireland is slightly overrepresented in relation to England, but the anomaly is nowhere near as great as in the cases of Scotland and Wales.

The multi-national character of the United Kingdom is not the only cause of a territorial barrier to fair representation. Johnston (1983: 14–15) produces evidence to suggest that the Commission staff divide up the country between them, and that no attempt is made to make consistent plans for the entire country. For example, he points to the contrasting fate of two similar cities, Oxford and Cambridge, in the 1982 reapportionment of seats – the former was split into two, predominantly urban, seats, while the latter retained one urban seat but had wards detached from the city and added to a primarily rural adjacent constituency. This piece-meal approach to constructing constituencies goes hand-in-hand with the Commission's mandate which is to use counties and London boroughs as the basic unit, so that constituencies cannot criss-cross county and borough boundaries, even if this would make for more equally sized constituencies. The result is a pronounced tendency to create compact constituencies where possible, and, since the Commission has no mandate to provide for representation for ethnic minorities, there are no British equivalents to the peculiarly-shaped Seventeenth District in New York.

In Britain constituency boundaries are moulded to the demands of the representation of persons, but, as the court case brought by the Labour party in 1983 revealed, it is places which are still represented: the Commissioners do not have to create absolutely equal constituencies, for they are required under the 1944 Act to pay attention to special geographic considerations. Indeed, quite explicitly in 1947 and

1955 the Commissioners created smaller constituencies in rural areas, because they claimed such constituencies were more difficult for their MPs to serve than were urban constituencies. In 1983 the Labour party argued that, with the proposed Surbiton constituency having an electorate of only 47,000 while the Isle of Wight would have one of 95,000, the Commissioners had failed to carry out their task of reapportionment adequately. But a court held that the statistical evidence did not show they had failed to carry out their statutory duty, and it pointed to the rule that the Commission cannot permit county and London borough boundaries to be crossed and that special geographical circumstances should be taken into account in the creation of constituencies.

By setting up a permanent Boundary Commission, the British Parliament ensured that its own members would not be involved directly in drawing up electoral districts. Even the debate on the Commissioners' report in the Commons has not been used so far as an opportunity for rewriting their proposals which the party possessing a Parliamentary majority has a reason to dislike. In this way what was a highly political activity in the nineteenth century, and remains so in much of the United States, has been partially de-politicized. Sometimes, in fact, those who want to reform the American procedures look at the British system as a possible model. However, the British procedures are far from being either unbiased or impossible to manipulate. This point is explained well by Muir and Paddison (1981: 107–8):

> In Britain, implementing the recommendations of the Boundary Commissioners has normally favoured the Conservative Party. As the ruling party has the option or not of actually introducing legislation adopting the Commissioners' recommendations, Labour governments (as in 1969) may be reluctant to introduce the changes; their failure to do so at that date, according to one estimate, gave them 11 extra seats.[7]

For all the political chicanery that can be involved with redistricting processes in the United States, there is one important advantage to the American approach. It recognizes explicitly that often there is no one obvious solution to the question of how to draw up electoral boundaries so as to allow votes to be translated into seats fairly. How you construct the boundaries will determine 'who gets what' in the political process – handing the task over to an impartial commission does not change this. Moreover, the use of such a commission tends to obscure the point, which is all too evident when electoral reapportionment is politicized, that reapportionment (as it is presently conducted in Britain and the

United States) does not aim to match overall votes to seats. Even if its results were to involve fewer biases than in the recent past, the British approach would still tend to disguise the way in which the representation of territory serves to compromise the democratic ideal of the representation of persons.

CONSEQUENCES OF TERRITORIAL REPRESENTATION

Until comparatively recently little attention was paid to the consequences for modern British politics of an electoral system which was territorially–based. There were two main reasons for this. There was a tendency still to see territorial representation as the 'normal' basis of elections – as Birch (1964: 228) noted, there has been no debate in Britain about the use of a party list system, which is the main practical alternative to territorial representation. More importantly, though, despite the use of territorial sub-units in elections, the British political system was mainly organized around functional representation – even in the House of Commons, where, in effect, from the 1920s until the 1960s, parties gained power through nationally based movements supporting them. There are, though, several important consequences for the British political system of having territorially based electoral 'units', and these consequences form the subject of this section.

The salience of political cleavages

In conjunction with plurality voting, territorial representation does affect the political divisions in a society. If all 650 MPs were elected on an individual basis in a single national constituency, then it is likely (from what we know about party loyalties among British voters) that all of them would be from one party – the party winning a plurality of votes. The division of voters into territorial sub-units makes it much more likely that some other parties will also be represented in the Commons; this is because there will be at least some constituencies where the distribution of voters (in terms of their interests) differs from the national profile.

In fact, there have been quite pronounced differences from one area to another – in particular, the Conservative party has always been relatively stronger in the south-eastern parts of England with the Labour party stronger in other parts of the country. Moreover, as Wood (1987: 394) could argue even before a 1987 election which continued this trend: 'The north–south and rural–urban divisions in British politics, always of relevance, have become more pronounced in the last seven elections compared with those before 1964.' But the crucial point to be made here is that territorial representation, at least with plurality voting, advantages only those interests which have concentrations of strength in particular locales. This point is most apparent when comparing the fortunes of the Labour and Alliance parties in the 1983 general election. The Labour party won 28 per cent of the vote and 209 seats, while the Alliance received 25 per cent of the vote but only twenty three seats (3.5 per cent of the total). The Labour party's voting strength was more concentrated in particular areas while, with the exception of the 'Celtic periphery', the Alliance strength was much more evenly distributed. (That third parties can flourish if they have a fairly strong regional base is well illustrated by Canada's New Democratic Party. It has polled between 16 and 20 per cent of the vote in every federal election since 1965, but it has never obtained less than 6.5 per cent of the Parliamentary seats, and in 1988 it got as much as 14 per cent of the seats. This is a much better ratio of seats to vote-share than the Liberal Democrats and their antecedents in Britain have obtained since the 1920s.)

The combination of plurality voting and territorial representation has been partly responsible for what some have argued has been the 'freezing of political cleavages' in Britain since the 1920s. The argument is that plurality voting puts pressure on British voters into choosing between one of the two largest parties – a vote for any other party would usually be little more than a protest against the alternatives offered by the two largest parties. Since the Labour party replaced the divided Liberal party as one of the two largest parties (after the 1918 elections) British politics has reflected a class cleavage which is articulated by Labour and the Conservatives. But, it is argued, as the social composition of Britain changed, it became difficult for new interests to be represented in parties which could challenge the Labour and Conservative parties, and so British politics continued to reflect the political divisions of the 1920s. But while attention is usually focused on the role of plurality voting in 'freezing' political divisions, the system of territorial representation is equally important. Because they were geographically dispersed, new social groups could not exert electoral power in the way that those mobilized in the Labour and Conservative parties could. Indeed, the form of territorial representation used in Britain actually accentuated the problems facing new political movements.

In considering this last point let us suppose that in 1982 Britain had created a single at-large constituency to replace the existing constituencies, and that just before the 1983 election the opinion polls showed the Alliance running neck-and-neck with the Labour party for second place. In a single national election, this information could be transmitted easily to the voters; any voter who wished to oppose the Conservative candidates could then decide where his or her vote might be placed to greatest effect. But with 650 constituencies it was far more difficult for the individual voter to understand how to use the vote to best effect. There are few reliable public opinion polls conducted at the constituency level in Britain, but, more importantly, making this information available to voters was virtually impossible. (This point is explored further in our consideration of 'political management' below.) Above the 'white noise' of the national campaigns, the voter could not be expected to take account and act on information relating purely to his or her constituency. Except in a few cases – such as those West Country seats where the Labour vote had already been much squeezed in the past by Liberal candidates – it became difficult for parties to get voters to act strategically. Thus, as in 1983, even if it were the case that a large number of voters were most concerned to vote against one party, it becomes much more difficult in elections based on small territorial units to organize them to use their votes most effectively – unless the parties collude with each other. As we shall see shortly, this problem is not always evident in by-elections, for many of the constraints of territorial representation evident in general elections are not found in by-elections.

But territorial representation affects the political significance of social cleavages in other ways too. For example, consider the division between the north and south of Britain which became yet more evident in the 1987 election. While support for the Conservative party declined significantly in the north in 1987, it increased throughout much of southern England. Now suppose this same election had been contested in a single national constituency. On the one hand, it can be argued that the result would not reveal so vividly regional differences in the distribution of the vote – there would be no pattern of seats for politicians and journalists to point to, but merely opinion poll evidence of voter support. In a sense, then, territorial representation helps to accentuate territorially–based political cleavages because it publicizes them. On the other hand, territorial representation may also reinforce such cleavages in that having MPs 'tied' to particular areas reduces the pressure on a party that there would be in a single national constituency to expand its electoral coalition to ensure victory at the next election. Because successful candidates and their local parties are likely to have more power within a party than unsuccessful ones, there is some tendency to consolidate support in their main areas of support rather than to broaden the electoral base. Because of territorial representation, there was a greater inclination in the Conservative party of the 1980s to 'forget' about the economically-declining north of the country; similarly, the Labour party found it more difficult to break away from its stronghold in the north to devise policies that were attractive to potential voters in the increasingly prosperous south. Of course, there have been pressures in both parties to move in these directions, but the point is that territorially–based representation in Parliament inevitably tends to act as a brake on such initiatives. Once again, we can see the conservatizing effects of this form of representation.

Moreover, we must not forget a point introduced earlier in the first section: territorial representation creates centres of power, which are especially useful for oppositions in mobilizing against interests that have access to the political system through functional representation. But the main sources of this power, of course, are not Parliamentary constituencies themselves but the local government units on which they have been based. Consequently, the centralization of authority which the Conservative governments of the 1980s attempted to bring about involved the dismantling of the powers of local governments, rather than plans to reform the territorial aspects of Parliamentary representation. Nevertheless, this territorial representation is not unimportant. Increasingly, MPs have had experience on local councils before being elected to the Commons, and while many candidates still do not have close ties with their constituencies before they are selected, there is still a significant minority of them with such ties – ties which today are more likely, especially outside the Conservative party, to include those to local authorities in their constituencies. Thus, changes in the patterns of the pre-Parliamentary political careers of MPs are tending to consolidate the territorial dimension of representation – and of opposition to functional interests whose power emanates from their links to government.

The 'representativeness' of representatives

If British Parliamentary candidates were chosen by their parties to contest an election in a single at-large constituency, it is almost certain that the 650 people elected would be a rather different group from those actually elected today. In some respects, though certainly not all, the candidates would probably be more representative of the electorate as a whole – in the sense that they shared certain characteristics of the voters. These are characteristics which in some ways are thought to be 'politically relevant'. In particular, there would be a great many more women candidates and probably a few more candidates from racial minorities. The reason for this is that in the single-member constituency system those involved in selecting candidates are especially vulnerable to the 'tyranny of small decisions': those involved in the process 'are obliged to make choices covering a range or a time span too small to take all relevant factors into account' (Hirsch 1977: 40). When a legislature is divided into single-member constituencies the task of selecting a candidate to fight a particular constituency usually falls to party elites within that constituency. Their responsibility is to select one candidate – they cannot influence the selection of candidates elsewhere, so that the only choice they can make is which candidate is best qualified overall to contest that particular seat.

Let us suppose that parties generally choose a candidate who has relevant political experience, and that historically more white, middle class males have had this experience than any other group in society, so that 90 per cent of the best-qualified candidates fall into this category. We may expect that about 90 per cent of constituency parties will choose a candidate from this group. As the number of people from other social groups with the relevant political experience increases slowly, so too will the number of Parliamentary candidates from these groups. However, what each of the local party elites is unlikely to do is ask – what is the best 'team' of candidates, in terms of the social groups represented in the 'team', for the party? The reason they do not ask this question is that, as individual local parties, they can do little to determine the overall composition of the 'team'. All they can do is select one candidate. Contrast this with the position of a party choosing an entire slate of 650 candidates. Even if 90 per cent of the best-qualified candidates are white middle class males, the party still has a choice as to whether it wants 90 per cent of its candidates to be of this type. It can decide that other considerations should be given weight – for instance, that the composition of the party's Parliamentary delegation should better reflect important characteristics of its voters. Such a party is not tyrannized by small units each taking a single decision about a candidate; instead, it can take a policy decision about its entire slate of candidates – and it has the means of implementing such a decision.

The impact that this aspect of constituency structure can have on change in party selection of candidates is illuminated by comparing the British and West German experiences. In Britain the proportion of MPs who are women remains small, and there is no evidence that it is likely to increase rapidly.[8] But in West Germany, where a party list system of voting is employed (albeit one organized at the regional – *Land* – level and not the national level), a policy decision by the Greens that at least

50 per cent of its Parliamentary delegation should be composed of women is effecting a much greater change. Subsequently the Social Democrats (SPD) have also had to commit themselves to greatly increasing the proportion of women Parliamentarians at both the federal and *Land* levels, and they have been able to effect this through the control of their party lists. As a result, while still under-represented in relation to men in the West German Parliaments, women are far less under-represented there than in the British House of Commons; in 1987 15 per cent of West German federal Parliamentarians were women while women MPs constituted only 6.3 per cent of the House of Commons (Lovenduski 1990: 149). (Of the liberal democracies, it is the Nordic countries where the parties have done most to ensure the political promotion of women (Lovenduski 1986: 154); as in West Germany, the Parliamentary representation of women has been facilitated by the use of party list systems.)

Single-member constituencies expose the problem of the tyranny of small decisions at its worst, but even in two- or three-member seats (of the kind common in Britain in the nineteenth century) it may still be difficult to change the overall composition of a Parliamentary delegation. For example, the larger the geographical area covered by a constituency, the more necessary it may be for electoral reasons to select representatives who live in different parts of the constituency. The need for 'geographical balance' of this kind may then make it difficult to achieve a balanced 'slate' with respect to characteristics such as race or sex. Once the number of seats contained in a single constituency becomes large, however, it is easier to achieve both 'geographical balance' and 'balance' in other respects as well. The easiest way, then, for a party to ensure that its delegation is composed as it would wish it to be composed is to have constituencies which are as large as possible – at best, a single national constituency.

Of course, it might be argued that this problem is of the parties' own making and not the product of a particular electoral system: after all, even in single-member constituencies, national parties could remove the power of nominating candidates from their local branches. But this is to ignore two factors. Not all parties are organized into branches which are subservient to the centre, but are more amalgams of local political notables; and, in any case, parties are unlikely to get the resources they need from the local level unless they cede some power, particularly influence over nominations, to that level. For example, arguably prime ministerial control over the party's Parliamentarians is even tighter in Canada than in Britain, yet the power of nominating candidates rests with the riding (constituency) associations.[9]

Nevertheless, the sceptic is right in suggesting that there are circumstances in which some kind of 'balance' can be introduced into a 'slate' of party representatives even with single-member constituencies. It is possible when there are a variety of offices to be contested at any one election. The classic example of this was in the United States in the late nineteenth and early twentieth centuries, where parties in urban areas, especially, sought to provide 'balanced tickets' – that is, a slate of candidates that contained members of different ethnic groups. If the Democratic gubernatorial candidate was an Irish– American, then it might be important to have an Italian–American, say, running for the congressional district on the same day, and perhaps a Jewish candidate for one of the state legislature seats. However, while this kind of 'balancing' could try to make the ticket appealing to all ethnic groups in one district, it could not affect the composition of the Democratic delegation in the House of Representatives – as in the British House of Commons, small decision-making prevented any 'balance' of this sort being attained.

Political management

In Britain territorial representation poses three kinds of problems of political management for parties – especially for the party which forms the government.

By-elections

When an election is contested on a purely national basis, the cost of holding another national election everytime a legislator dies or resigns is so large that vacancies have to be filled in some other way. For example, in the case of a party list system the party which has lost a member from the legislature can nominate a replacement. In fact, there is nothing to stop such a practice being used in elections based on territorial units, but in practice by-elections (or special elections, as they are called in the United States) are usually employed. The reason for this is that, since territorial legislative representation originated in Britain and representation here preceded the rise of parties, many countries using this form of representation have followed the older British practice.[10]

Until the mid twentieth century by-elections were of relatively limited political significance. There were two reasons for this. First, as it happened, for many decades following the rise of tightly organized Parliamentary parties (in the last quarter of the nineteenth century) the balance of power in Parliament did not hinge on the results of by-elections. It was not until 1950 that a Parliament was elected where the ability of the governing party to manage the Commons might have been affected directly by by-election results. In fact, the 1950–1 Parliament was dissolved before any by-election could be held. However, both the 1964–6 and 1974–9 Labour governments had such small majorities that any change in the composition of the Commons would affect the party's ability to manage Parliamentary affairs. Indeed, the Labour government elected in October 1974 had lost sufficient seats in by-elections by 1977 that it was forced into a pact with the Liberal party in order to remain in office. Secondly, the advent of television, which could be seen in only a tiny minority of homes before the 1950s, but which was accessible to most people by the end of that decade, changed the role of by-elections. National attention could now be focused on virtually any by-election – turning many of them into informal tests of a government's popularity. But it is not only the governing party that may find themselves under pressure in a by-election – the failure to hold one of its seats may help to undermine the credibility of an opposition party.

One clear instance of the latter was the Bermondsey by-election in 1983 when the Labour party lost the seat to the Liberals; three months later a general election was held, and the timing of that election by the Conservative government owed much to the evidence of weakness in Labour party support which the Bermondsey by-election had exposed. This example also illustrates an important difference between a general election fought in territorially–based constituencies and a by-election fought under such a system. Today media attention focused on a by-election makes it much easier for parties to induce strategic voting than is possible in a general election. In Bermondsey opinion poll evidence during the campaign showed that the Conservatives had little hope of winning, and the publicity given to this produced a late swing in support to the Liberals – the only party that might defeat the Labour candidate. In a general election this kind of detailed information about voter opinion would be unlikely to be available, but, even if it were, convincing the voters of the situation would be virtually impossible amidst the 'white noise' of the national campaign and the national opinion polls.[11]

By-elections, then, introduce a somewhat arbitrary factor into the process of political management. Often their timing cannot be controlled – as in cases of death and political disgrace, and also when Parliamentarians pursue new careers – so that by-elections may coincide with particularly opportune or inopportune circumstances for a party.[12] Moreover, because the constituencies involved may be highly unrepresentative in certain respects, the indication they give about party fortunes may be unclear. It is useful, perhaps, to compare their role with that of *Land* elections in West Germany, which also give indications of popular support for national parties but which involve fewer random elements. Here too sub-national elections are used by both parties and media as gauges of party popularity, and as with by-elections local circumstances may make such tests misleading. But, unlike by-elections, they cannot make government directly unviable for a party, they involve many more voters, and they are not the product of freak political circumstances – such as the death of a particular person.

The Scottish dimension

Scotland has its own legal system and (since 1885) its own Secretary of State who has responsibility for various areas of administration which are the responsibility of other government departments in the rest of the UK. Parliamentary posts in the Scottish Office have to be filled, although Peers may be used as well as MPs, and there is a Scottish Grand Committee which deals with the Committee stage of bills relating to Scotland. Traditionally Scottish MPs have constituted a large majority of the members of this committee, and the ethos of the Commons has been that Scottish business is business for Scots' representatives alone; as John Mackintosh (1967: 391) noted about the stages of a Scottish bill: 'any English MP who might have the temerity to speak would be regarded with a mixture of horror and fury by Scots MPs on both sides'. This approach to management of the Commons posed no problems so long as the major parties continued to win an adequate number of seats each in Scotland. In 1987, though, Conservative support in Scotland collapsed and the party won only ten seats. Not only did this pose difficulties for the composition of the Scottish Grand Committee, it also posed intractable problems in relation to the Scottish Affairs Select Committee. Like other Commons' Select Committees, the latter was composed of backbenchers and it investigated aspects of the work of a particular government department – in this case the Scottish Office. Unlike other Select Committees, though, membership had been determined on a territorial basis – only MPs for Scottish constituencies sat on it. Although the Opposition was willing to reduce the size of the Scottish Affairs Committee, it proved impossible to re-establish this Committee after the 1987 election because of the small Scottish Conservative representation in the Commons. This problem could never have arisen, of course, in a non-territorial electoral system.

Regional legitimacy

Does the emergence of strong regional patterns of voter support under a system of territorially–based elections reduce the legitimacy of a governing party in an area where it has little support? This was a problem which increasingly faced Liberal governments in Canada, especially after the 1980 election. In 1980 the Liberals won a Parliamentary majority but obtained only two of the seventy-seven seats in the four western provinces. This increased western alienation from Ottawa. In Britain too there has been a marked regional pattern of support for parties throughout the whole era of liberal democratic politics. The Conservative party has been primarily an *English* party in terms of its support, and it has been especially strong in south-east England; its opponents have drawn disproportionately on support elsewhere. Until the 1980s, though, significant pockets of voter support outside their areas of greatest strength meant that governing parties had no problem in claiming a national mandate to enact their policies.[13] Of course, until 1989 neither the Conservative nor the Labour parties had organizations in Northern Ireland, although the Conservatives have now changed tack, so there could have been no question of a mandate from that province.

In the 1980s, however, these regional voting patterns became more pronounced. We have just noted the collapse of Conservative representation in Scotland in 1987 and at the same election the Labour party's competitiveness in much of south-east England continued to weaken. But do these developments erode a government's claim to have a national mandate? Certainly, the results in Scotland seem to have stimulated nationalistic sentiments again, but there is little evidence that there has been a widespread increase in the belief that the Conservative government is an illegitimate government for Scotland because of its lack of support there. As we write, it is unclear whether even the introduction of the unpopular poll tax in Scotland, preceding its introduction in England and Wales, will prompt widespread civil disobedience in the form of non-payment of the tax.[14] Compliance would reflect the successful, if partial, integration of the Scottish nation into the United Kingdom over a period of nearly 300 years.

Yet, quite clearly, experience from other countries does suggest that lack of a territorial base in a particular region can help to undermine a government's legitimacy, but much depends on how a government responds to that regime. For example, the rise of the Republican party in the mid 1850s prompted fears among whites in the American south that its own interests would be threatened should the Republicans win the Presidency and control of Congress. Indeed, Lincoln's victory in 1860 did provoke secession and a civil war. After the war and the Reconstruction period, however, the South could 'live with' Republican administrations in Washington because they made no efforts to interfere with white control of the South. While a second civil war would have been impossible, forms of civil disobedience directed against the federal government may well have emerged if a more interventionist style had been adopted. But the US example exposes the influence of one institutional device for coping with a territorially–based legitimacy crisis which is not available in Britain – federalism. In the United States in the late nineteenth century, as in Canada in the late twentieth century, the availability of powerful political units below the level of the national government could facilitate the short-term accommodation of regional alienation from the dominant party at the national level.

It may be surmised, then, that in Britain the problem of legitimacy would arise only if a government persisted in seeking to impose, on a region in which it lacked support, policies that quite clearly ran counter to the interests of that particular region. At the moment there is scant evidence of such developments.

The representation of local interests

Representation on the basis of territorial sub-units makes it more likely representatives will be engaged in the promotion of local interests than would occur with non-territorial representation. But if an electoral system of the Anglo-American kind can facilitate the access of local interests to the policy making process it does not guarantee it. Until the 1960s political scientists had no hesitation in drawing a stark contrast between Britain and the United States in this regard. In the United States legislators were locally based politicians – the absence of a strong connection with his or her district was an electoral liability for a candidate. Candidates depended as much on their own efforts in securing re-election as on the fortunes of their party; and to secure their own electoral future, many of them sought to advance (through legislation and advocacy) the interests of their constituents. At its strongest, this form of representation entailed 'pork-barrel' politics – the use of voting power in the legislature to secure benefits for individual constituencies that could not be justified in terms of national policy priorities. As Brams (1976: 108) notes of the United States Congress:

One can see ... the process at work in, for example, the rivers and harbors bills of the twentieth century when they ceased to have the character of vital internal improvements that they had had in the nineteenth century. A majority gain from the pork in such barrels, else the bills would not pass. But there are also losses, external costs.

By contrast, British legislators were entirely at the mercy of national political trends. Those from safe constituencies would always be re-elected, while those in marginal constituencies could expect to lose their seats whenever there was a national swing of sufficient size. The link between Parliamentary candidates, at least those standing in winnable seats, and their constituencies was weak – most were neither residents of their constituencies nor had any other connection with them.[15] Even after their election to Parliament, many MPs did not live in their constituencies. With a few exceptions, such as in some of the rural seats in Wales and Scotland, there was only a small 'personal' vote, so that an MP had little incentive to devote much time to constituency affairs or to promote constituency interests. In brief, the territorial basis of representation in the British case had only a small impact on the way in which representatives acted. In Rose's (1982: 88) words:

> Party competition emphasizes functional or class loyalties, not geographical loyalties. More than 95 per cent of all MPs (and until the breakaway of Ulster Unionists from the Conservatives in 1972, more than 99 per cent) are elected as representatives of British parties divided by functional interests.

While a comparison of Britain and the United States today emphasizing the points just made would not be wholly inaccurate, there have been a number of important changes in the character of territorial representation in Britain. Swings in British general elections have become increasingly non-uniform since 1964: an MP can no longer predict with accuracy the likely effect a national swing of x per cent against his or her party will have on his or her own seat. This does not mean, though, that there has been a great increase in the ability of individual MPs to control their electoral fortunes. There are many factors affecting re-election chances which the MP cannot influence directly. For example, gentrification in some inner-London constituencies in the 1980s was bound to make some Labour seats that much more difficult to hold in the 1987 election however much the national performance of the party improved after 1983. But in a less predictable political universe candidates, especially those in constituencies which are, or may become, marginal, are more likely to turn to activities that may increase their chances of re-election. To counter adverse party swings in their area they must look to ways of increasing their *personal* vote – a strategy which is at the very heart of American electoral politics.

There are, of course, many ways of stimulating a personal vote in the United States that are simply unavailable to a British MP. Strict limitations on campaign spending in Britain, together with the small size of constituencies in relation to media markets, make it far more difficult for most MPs to make their names familiar among their constituents. Nearly all legislation of any importance is government-sponsored legislation, so that apart from a few isolated exceptions such as David Alton in the case of abortion, there are no instances of MPs gaining enormous publicity through the initiation of legislation. In the United States, of course, claiming credit for particular items of legislation is one of the key elements of a legislator's electoral strategy. Nevertheless, there are two ways in which the MP can try to build up personal support.

The first is through constituency service in the role which Searing (1985) called 'welfare officers'. In this role the MP attends to the need of individual constituents – referring those contacting him or her to relevant officials, when appropriate, or interceding with local or central government departments when necessary. As has long been recognized in the United States, the need for 'troubleshooters' to whom individual citizens can turn increased as the state's responsibilities for the economy and for welfare provision increased. Elected public officials – at local or national level – are well placed to act as 'troubleshooters' because often they have privileged access to the officials who can resolve the issues. Although in his study of the early 1970s Searing found that the extent of constituency service by MPs was not related to their electoral vulnerability, a more recent study suggests this may have changed and that those representing marginal constituencies are the most likely to be active in this way (Cain *et al.* 1983).

The second way in which an MP can seek to build up 'personal' electoral support is through lobbying for interests that are important to his or her constituency. Of course, the boundary between the territorial manifestations of a functional interest and an interest that is primarily territorial in character is often difficult to determine (Wood 1987). However, there are many interests which are territorial: the privatiz-ation of Devonport dockyard, the location of a new London airport, and policies for new housing development in south-eastern England would all be examples of this. As with the 'welfare officer' role, there is evidence of increasing activity by MPs in representing local interests. As Wood (1987: 409) concluded from his study of Conservative MPs:

The 'territorial imperative' has not as yet manifested itself to any great extent in the division lobbies, but the evidence that local industries are a preoccupation of numerous MPs, especially those representing areas where jobs are in jeopardy, is readily available from an examination of debates and of oral and written questions.

For a variety of reasons – the absence of the separation of powers, and the presence of nationally-based parties included – British MPs are never going to come close to emulating American legislators in terms of a constituency orientation. Most especially, it must be remembered that the dominance of functional representation in Britain both within Parliament and through direct links between dominant economic interests and government constrains the part that territorial representation can play. Nevertheless, there is evidence that, as the rigidly 'national' political universe of the period 1918–64 is eroding, so the opportunity for greater territorial representation by MPs increases. While there is precious little 'pork' to sustain 'pork barrel' politics in Britain, there are still a number of areas in resource allocation in which MPs can intervene to gain special treatment for constituencies.

CONCLUDING REMARKS

In this chapter we have compared the idea of territorial representation with the idea of functional representation. This led us to consider whether there were any good arguments for an exclusively territorial system of representation. We discovered that, while there is a case for some territorial representation, an exclusively territorial system could not be justified. The principle which was earlier identified as potentially in conflict with territorial representation is that persons should be represented – the implications of which were explored in Chapter 4.

Because the use of a plurality voting system in electing a body of representatives is so often conjoined with territorial representation, there is always a risk that the territorial elements of a voting system will be overlooked. In this chapter we have suggested that the organization of Parliamentary elections on a territorial basis does have consequences for the way the British political system works. Moreover, if the role of the European Parliament in policy-making increases in the future, we may expect that the territorial basis of British representation in that body will also affect the nature of representation there. That the British organize their elections in geographically defined constituencies is not a minor piece of political detail – it certainly does affect 'who gets what' from the policy-making process.

The precise mechanics of any electoral system have an effect on 'who gets what' and in the next chapter we shall be examining a number of alternative electoral systems which have found favour with political scientists or regimes. In our review of those systems we shall return to the problem of balancing the element of territorial representation with the element of personal representation involved in each system.

7 Aggregating votes
Rival systems

INTRODUCTION

This chapter is devoted to the dispute about the 'best' system of voting, a dispute which can be approached in two very different ways.[1] The first approach raises an abstract theoretical question: given the properties of various voting systems, is one clearly 'the best', and on what basis do we evaluate them to decide? The second approach is more practical: would the overall shape of the political system under a different electoral system to that currently employed in Britain be preferable? Of course, if we can identify the 'best' system, we seem to have an answer to the practical question. But there are good reasons for trying to answer the question in the abstract, before thinking about the consequences of adopting another electoral system in Britain.

It was pointed out earlier that a good deal of discussion in Britain has been about the rival merits of plurality voting and proportional representation, and much of it has been mere speculation about the results of elections had some sort of PR system been in operation. There are two limitations attached to this sort of speculation. First, as we explained in Chapter 1,[2] assumptions have to be made about how voters would have cast their ballots under a different voting system. While it is implausible to suppose that everybody would have voted in the same way (because of changed strategic considerations), it is difficult to obtain definite information about how the voting pattern would have been affected. The problem is exacerbated by the reasonable expectation that many other aspects of political practice would be likely to alter if the voting system did. In particular, voters' attitudes towards potential coalition governments would usually be important. This is why the counterfactual exercise is essentially speculative.

The second limitation on this approach is that it is often concerned solely with whether particular parties would improve their Parliamentary position under the PR version. This is undoubtedly an important consideration for the parties themselves, and there are disputes within those parties as to whether PR would be 'a good thing' given the expected pattern of support achieved. But when we ask whether, in the abstract, one voting system is better than another, we shall want to take many more factors than the interests of existing parties into account. Indeed, as we shall see, we might be aiming for a voting system which was neutral (in a sense to be explained) between them.

Having distinguished the theoretical issue (is there an ideal voting system?) from the practical issue (how might we expect British political practice to be altered by a change in the voting system?) we shall begin by trying to answer the theoretical question. We must first recall that not all systems of voting are designed to elect a representative assembly, so our question must be refined to ask whether there is an ideal voting system to achieve that objective. But as we saw in Chapter 4, representation may be construed in a number of different ways, and it may be a voting system which seems appropriate to achieve one sort of representativeness fails to produce another sort. We must therefore be alert to these complexities, which involve judgements about what sort of political practice is most democratic. The electoral system 'meshes' with other aspects of political activity, and it is impossible to divorce a judgement about the democratic character of the electoral system from a judgement about the polity in which it is embedded.

The subject of this chapter relates to the aggregation of votes. This element of an electoral system links two of the 'phases' identified by Rae, namely ballot structure and electoral formulae (Rae 1971). In Rae's typology, an electoral formula refers to the rules used to translate votes into seats. But, of course, as students of electoral systems, we are interested not only in such formulae, but also in the question of how votes are treated at the point at which they are added up.

We shall therefore organize this part of the discussion as follows. First, we isolate the basic variable elements in electoral systems. Secondly, we consider the systems popular today. Thirdly, we discuss some of the problems of preference aggregation. Finally, we examine a proposal about how an ideal system should be identified.

BASIC VARIABLES IN ELECTORAL SYSTEMS

There is an indefinite number of possible systems of voting, and the mathematical study of their properties has become a highly technical pursuit (for example, Sugden 1981: Chapter 8). But we may begin with a simple distinction between two elements of the way in which elections are conducted. The first element is the information the voter is able to record; the second element is the way in which the information is treated. We are initially concerned, in other words, with the voter's expression of preference(s) and the process by which the preferences of the voters are aggregated.

An individual voter is asked to express preferences between candidates. There are many ways in which voting systems differ, and many ways of classifying those differences, but amongst the variable elements of the way in which these preferences may be expressed which seem most important are the following.

The extent of the voter's choice

Some electoral systems provide that the voter can write the name of someone for whom he or she wishes to express a preference on the ballot paper. Such a system gives the voter greater choice, so the question of whether writing-in is possible is part of a wider issue about the extent of the choice the voter has available, an important consideration in evaluating the contribution of the electoral system to the democratic character of the polity. Of course, we should not assume that the number of choices available is an adequate measure of the value of choice, since, for example, a choice between five candidates all sponsored by the same political party may be less valuable to the voter than a choice between four very different candidates.

How many choices is the voter allowed?

Systems vary in the number of distinct choices the voter is being asked to make. For example, a system which aims to select two officeholders from a list of five candidates may require the voter to express positive support for one or two of the candidates, while another system may be constructed so that the voter is asked to name only one chosen candidate.

Is the voter asked to vote for a party or for individual candidates?

As we shall see below, in a strict party list system, the voter has no control over which individual candidate benefits from the vote he or she casts. This is in a sense the opposite case to the availability of the write-in option, since the pure party list system excludes voting for individuals while the write-in system facilitates it. But absence of choice of individual beneficiary is compatible with great choice between parties.

Is the voter able to rank the candidates?

The plurality system of voting asks only that a cross be put against the name of the most-favoured candidate (or party). The voter's preference between the candidates who are not his or her first choice is not recorded. Other voting systems require or allow a preference ordering by which the voter can provide an ordinal ranking of preference, either from 1 to n, where n is the number of candidates, or from 1 to $n\text{-}x$, for example when the voter is asked to name in order of preference three of ten candidates.

Is the voter able to record the intensity of preferences?

Some voting systems have been designed in the hope of allowing voters to express the intensity of their preferences between candidates (or parties). Such a system would allow the voter to say not only (for example) that Leftwing is preferred to Middleman who is preferred to Rightwing, but also by how much. One example was discussed earlier, in Chapter 2.[3] Another example might ask the elector to award each candidate points out of ten, so the voter recorded, say, Leftwing 10, Middleman 4, Rightwing 1. But how are these numbers to be interpreted? They *might* be taken to imply that intensity of the voter's preference for Leftwing over Middleman was greater than the intensity of his or her preference for Middleman over Rightwing, since the 'gaps' on the preference scale are 6 units and 3 units; but as ratios, the relationships are 2.5:1 and 4:1, suggesting that the preference for Middleman over Rightwing is stronger than the preference for Leftwing over Middleman. Even if this information is recorded, there will be a problem of comparability between any two voters. Two scores of 8 recorded by different individuals may well represent different levels of preference or expected utility.

Is abstention a positive option?

In most voting systems, it is possible not to vote. But the information that can be conveyed by non-participation is rather less than can be conveyed by a positive registration of the unacceptability of some or all of the candidates. Non-voting may be treated as indifference, as alienation, or as satisfaction with any outcome, but some systems allow for participation to be coupled with a rejection of all candidates. For example, a voting system might allow the elector to cross out the names of candidates who were not acceptable, and it would then make a difference if a ballot in which all names were deleted was treated as spoilt, and not counted, or whether all the negative votes were counted.[4]

Mechanisms for aggregating the preferences expressed by individual voters also exhibit some important differences, to which we may return when we have examined some of the systems proposed or in use. As a preliminary, we may consider the following schedule of preferences and the way in which different aggregation procedures will produce different winners. All of the procedures allow the voters to provide more information about their preferences than the British plurality system. Three candidates (*ABC*) are competing for one office; five voters (*VWXYZ*) are asked to rank the three candidates in order of preference.

	V	W	X	Y	Z
1	A	B	C	B	C
2	B	C	A	C	A
3	C	A	B	A	B

One aggregation procedure would look at the first preferences, of which there are two for *B*, two for *C* and one for *A*. If *A* were therefore eliminated, and *V*'s vote transferred to his or her second preference, *B*, then *B* would have a majority. An alternative aggregation procedure would be to award points according to the preference information. This would typically be done by giving 2 points for a first preference, 1 for a second preference and none for the last. On this basis, *A* would receive 4 points, *B* would receive 5 points and *C* 6 points, and *C* would be elected. Although the information voters have provided is exactly the same in the two cases, the difference in the method of aggregation employed leads to a different result. So we have to decide which is more important: to give first preferences particular weight, but to allow subsequent preferences to come into play for those voters whose first choice is eliminated, or to take all preferences into account from the start. But this is only an example, and we may now proceed to look at the mechanics of the electoral systems which have attracted support.

POPULAR ELECTORAL SYSTEMS

The single-member plurality system

This is, of course, the system currently employed in the United Kingdom's Parliamentary elections. Voters are asked to indicate which of the candidates they most prefer, and the aggregation procedure is simply an addition of these first preferences. The candidate with the most first preference support is elected. If there is a tie, the choice between the tied candidates is left to chance. Voters are not asked about their preferences for candidates other than their first choice. There is no procedure for aggregating a pattern of preferences across constituency boundaries (other than the composition of Parliament). The winner takes all in two senses: only the victor in any particular constituency benefits from the votes cast in his or her (or his or her party's) favour, and the party with the largest number of constituency winners is usually invited to form a government. We have already seen that the plurality winner in a particular constituency need not be a majority winner; and the party with the largest number of seats need not have secured a plurality, much less a majority, of votes cast, and certainly not of the electorate as a whole.

A standard criticism of the plurality system is that votes are 'wasted'. There are two cases to consider. In the first case, a voter might have a genuine first preference for a minority party which has no chance of victory in that particular constituency. To vote for the party will register support, but since there is no mechanism by which this voter's support can be aggregated with that of voters elsewhere in the country, it has no effect on the composition of the representative assembly. In the second case, polarities in political support lead to massive majorities, so a successful candidate achieves not only the necessary plurality but a considerable 'excess' majority. These additional votes are allegedly 'wasted' in the sense that they are not necessary to elect this candidate, but cannot be used in support of anyone else of the same political persuasion. One problem, then, is that votes for unsuccessful candidates are non-additive; the other problem is that the extra and unneeded votes for successful candidates are not transferable.

The multi-member plurality system

The plurality system may be modified to take account of the need to elect more than one representative for a particular constituency. This might be done by allowing each voter one vote, and declaring the necessary number of candidates elected who receive the most votes, or by allowing each voter a number of votes and proceeding in the same way. The former version is referred to as the single non-transferable vote system. Again, the difference between the multi-member plurality system in which each voter has more than one vote, and the single non-transferable vote procedure, could prove important, as the following example illustrates.

	V	W	X	Y	Z
1	A	B	C	B	C
2	B	C	A	A	A
3	C	A	B	C	B

This schedule gives the voters' actual preferences. If each is allowed one vote, and two candidates are to be elected, A will receive one vote, B two and C two; hence B and C will be chosen. But if each voter is allowed two separate votes, and we assume that they all cast one vote for their most favoured candidate and one for their second choice, then A will top the poll! As Urwin explains (1987b: 12), multi-member plurality systems and single non-transferable vote systems require different strategies from parties.

The Borda Count

The Borda Count is in fact the second system of aggregation used in the example of the consequences of aggregation procedures introduced above. Voters are asked to list their preference ranking from 1 to n, where n is the number of candidates, and n-1 points are awarded to first choices, n-2 to second choices and so on. Although n-1, n-2 and so on is the usual implementation of Borda's proposal, the formal requirement of a Borda Count is that the points' interval between successive rankings be equal. (When that requirement is fulfilled, the Borda Count will produce the same winner, whether the points be, for example, 2,1,0 or 6,4,2.) The points are then totalled, and the candidate with the greatest number of points is elected.

But what do these numbers represent? There is a certain arbitrariness about the points system employed. Looking at the schedule of preferences laid out above, we can see that if we proceed as Borda suggested, and gave a first preference 2 points, a second 1 and a third none, A would receive 5 points, B 5 and C 5, suggesting that the electorate supported all three candidates in equal measure. But if we adopted similar procedures (which do not meet Borda's requirement), giving a first preference 6 points, a second 3 and a third 1, the result would be A 16, B 17 and C 17, suggesting that A was least favoured, while if it were 3, 2 and 0 points B and C would look least favoured, receiving 8 points to A's 9. This is why the relative weights attached to each level of preference remain important even if the voter is allowed to express a full ranking of preferences. In this example, the question of who came last might affect the outcome through the procedure for resolving a tie.

Since the voter is recording only a ranking, and conveys nothing about the intensity of his or her preferences, we do not know what numbers to attach to any particular rank, nor have we any reason to suppose that such numbers would be the same for all voters. It is not intuitively obvious why we should prefer Borda's own specification of the points to be awarded to any other.

Condorcet's criterion

In Chapter 3, we introduced the idea of a Condorcet winner.[5] This requires that, if one candidate in an election could beat every other candidate in a head-to-head contest, then that candidate should be elected. In the schedule of preferences shown on page 146, in the second section, there is no Condorcet winner. In a two-way contest between A and B, A would win; in a similar contest between A and C, C would win; and finally B would beat C in such a contest. Thus although Condorcet's criterion specifies an appealing condition for electoral victory, it is insufficient in some cases to identify a winner.

Approval voting

Approval voting was mentioned in Chapter 1.[6] Under this procedure, each voter is given as many votes as there are candidates. The voters can cast only one vote each per candidate, but they may vote for as many candidates as they wish. To vote for every candidate would not contribute to the result. The point of approval voting is to enable voters to indicate which candidates they do *not* wish to be elected. The information revealed by the preference schedule on page 148 does not allow us to predict how voters employing approval voting would behave. Let us suppose, however, that each of the voters would not 'approve' of his or her least-favoured candidate. On that assumption, A would win the election with four votes, while B and C would receive only three votes each.

The Alternative Vote

This is the other system used in the preliminary example. It aims to produce a majority winner by examining the first preferences of the voters. If a candidate has an overall majority, he or she is elected; if not, the candidate receiving the least number of first preferences is eliminated, and votes cast in his or her favour are transferred to each voter's second-choice candidate. The process is repeated until someone achieves a majority. If it is necessary to eliminate several candidates, a particular voter's third or lower preference might be counted. This system does not take account of the ranking unless a candidate is eliminated, and it then accords the same status to a lower-preference vote as it does to a first-preference vote.

Two-stage or 'run-off' systems

Urwin identifies a number of different examples of run-off systems; what they have in common is the need for a second round if no-one achieves a majority on the first round (1987b: 30). They differ in the stipulations attached to the qualifications to enter the second round – from the case in which only the top two candidates in the first round are allowed to proceed, guaranteeing (saving the case of a tie) that one will receive a majority of votes cast, to cases in which all previous contestants, and new ones, may enter the second round, which is then decided by a plurality.

The single transferable vote

The STV combines some features of the alternative vote, in its elimination procedure, with the special feature of potentially redistributing some votes from candidates who are elected. It relies on defining a quota of votes which someone must receive in order to be elected. John Stuart Mill was a great admirer of what he referred to as 'Hare's scheme' (Mill 1910: 261–7); and Hare was proposing the use of a particular formula for determining the quota. Hare defined the quota as

$$\frac{\text{total number of votes}}{\text{total number of seats}}$$

but the formula now used, for example in the Irish Republic, is

$$\left[\frac{\text{total number of votes}}{(\text{total number of seats} + 1)} \right] + 1$$

Since Mill was particularly concerned about the dangers of oppressive majorities, we shall want to consider this aspect of PR systems in more detail later, when we deal with the evaluation of voting systems from criteria derived from a commitment to democracy.

In an STV system, each voter records his or her preference ranking of the candidates (or of as many as he or she wishes to include). The quota system works only if there is more than one seat per constituency. STV is compatible with territorial representation. There is no difficulty in arranging for the representation of particular constituencies, provided that there is more than one representative per constituency.

After the voters have recorded their preference rankings, the first preferences are counted, just as they are under the Alternative Vote system. On a first count, the quota (however defined) will either be met by one or more candidates, or it will not be achieved by anyone. If a candidate does achieve the quota, he or she is of course elected. But the quota defines a figure which is sufficient for election: if the candidate has received more votes than the quota, the 'surplus' is redistributed. It is redistributed to the other candidates in proportion to the ratios of the second preferences of all the votes cast for the individual in question. In other words, the system does not identify certain votes as 'surplus' and then reallocate according to the second preferences of those particular voters. Rather, it reallocates the extra votes by looking at the second preferences of everyone who supported the elected candidate, and adding to the first preferences of the other candidates a proportion of the extra votes determined by the pattern of second preferences.

If no-one achieves the quota, then the Alternative Vote rule applies: the candidate with the least number of first preferences drops out, and the votes for that person are redistributed. Since these are specifically identifiable, they are redistributed according to the second preferences specified by the voters.

After the first evaluation of the votes, one or other of these two possibilities will lead to a new set of totalled votes for each candidate, and the same rules can be re-applied in successive rounds until the required number of successful candidates are elected. With the preference schedule on both pages 146 and 148, B and C would be elected in a two-member constituency.

The key features of this system reproduce some of those of the alternative vote: if elector X votes for an eliminated candidate his or her further preferences are still taken into account, even though this may mean that his or her second, third, fourth (or whatever) preference is ranked equally with voter Y's first preference. Additionally, the preferences of voters beyond their first choice are taken into account in the sense that no candidate has a surplus of votes since the extra ones are proportionally redistributed. Both points are usually summarized in the claim that the STV system eliminates 'wasted' votes.

Party list systems

This is a class of systems whose special feature is the role of the parties in presenting lists of candidates to the voters. The effect of these party lists is to rank the party's order of preference among the candidates, so that an individual voter, in casting a vote for that party, will simply be allocating his or her vote to whomever is next on the party list. The dominance of the party's preference ranking may, however, be somewhat diluted by the precise mechanism chosen, and Urwin provides the following example in which the dilution is considerable:

> In the first instance, the voter is not restricted to a single party list. Consequently, therefore he must have *more than one vote*, at the extreme having as many votes as there are seats. The extreme case (Switzerland) also means full freedom to use these votes as he desires. In a ten seat constituency, for example, he may give a single vote to each of the ten candidates, irrespective of their party affiliation. He may divide his ten votes among three or four candidates from the same or different parties, or he may give all his votes to a single candidate.
>
> (Urwin 1977: 21)

Urwin's classification of electoral systems divides party list types into two main variants: the highest average and various remainder systems. The objective of the highest average systems is that as the process of allocation proceeds, the seat next to be allocated should go to the party which has the highest average of votes. The most commonly used method was named after the Belgian mathematician, d'Hondt. The remainder systems work by allocating the seats per constituency according to a quota, and then by allocating remaining seats according to the votes 'left over' after the quota has been applied. The remaining seats could be given to the parties with the greatest number of leftover votes, or the least number, and in principle in several other ways.

There are other complicating factors in the systems actually employed in electing representatives. Some systems have a qualifying percentage of the vote cast before a party will qualify for any seats at all; and this threshold itself varies. (In West Germany, which now employs the Nimeyer version of the remainder system, the threshold is 5 per cent.) Other systems allow for 'bonus' seats for the largest party. But even this brief discussion of some of the mechanisms which have been suggested or used for aggregating votes puts us in a better position to identify the variable features. Coupling this with the variables we noted in the expression of individual preferences will enable us to consider what might be the relevant considerations in choosing an electoral system.

Does the system preserve the preference rankings of the voter?

We have seen that the Borda Count aggregates all the preferences of all the voters. The points system takes into account, but gives a lower status to, second and lower preferences. The alternative vote and STV take account of lower preferences in some circumstances, but have to treat a voter's current highest preference as a first preference, even if it is in fact a fourth choice.

We might also ask, of those cases in which the voter has more than one vote, like the multi-member plurality system and the Swiss version of the party list system described above, whether the different votes can be deployed to convey preference information. The multi-member multiple-vote plurality system in effect counts two (or more) votes as equal first preferences, even though the voter may conceive those votes as ranked preferences. Indeed, the voter might prefer, what the aggregation procedure does not allow, to give two votes to one of the candidates, as the Swiss system would permit.

Do all votes count equally?

This is one of the most hotly disputed issues in the argument between supporters of the merits of different electoral systems. But it is also a complex question, and some of the heat arises because protagonists are at cross-purposes about what the question is asking. It is therefore wise to distinguish between some alternative ways of interpreting it. One narrow way of treating it is to assume it is asking only whether all voters bring the same resources to the election, before anyone actually votes. In this way the answer to the question will always be yes, whatever the procedure, provided that all voters have equal resources. They are all equally placed, with respect to the aggregation procedure, before they begin to use it, because they all have votes which *have the potential* to be taken into account when they are cast. For example, under plurality voting, all votes count equally in this narrow sense, even the votes of those persons about to abstain. Of course, variations in constituency size mean that, strictly speaking, a voter in a constituency with a smaller electorate is deploying a slightly larger resource compared to a voter in a larger constituency, even though in both cases there is equality within the particular constituencies.

A second way of interpreting the question is to think of it as a question about the impartiality with which the procedure is applied. Clearly, if there is corruption so some votes are ignored, perhaps by destroying some votes or treating them as spoiled ballots when they are unambiguous, then all votes are not counted equally. However, a comparison of the formal properties of electoral systems will have to assume honest and impartial use of the system, except if there could be an argument that some systems are more vulnerable to corruption by officials than others. A slightly different problem is whether some systems are more liable to strategic voting than others, and whether the degree of that vulnerability should be a consideration in selecting a system.

To avoid these two legitimate but unhelpful interpretations, we might refine the question a little, to ask whether the voters' preferences count equally. Here again, though, we shall need to consider three different bases on which an answer might be given. First, we might want to know whether each voter's set of preferences counts equally. This will resolve itself into either of the first two interpretations of the general question, above, in which case we are no further forward, or one of the other two interpretations of the refined question. These are: are equal preferences counted equally, and does each voter equally contribute to or determine the outcome of the election?

Clearly the plurality system can claim to count equal preferences equally, in the limited sense that each voter is allowed to express one preference and all those (first) preferences are added up. But since the aggregation procedure relies on excluding other preference information, this is rather like giving everyone equal respect by showing it to no-one. In systems that allow for the expression of more than one preference, equal ranked preferences will not necessarily be treated in the same way. The Borda Count does treat all first preferences alike, all second (and subsequent) preferences alike, in its system for awarding points. But STV and the alternative vote work by treating some voters' second (or subsequent) preferences as on a par with other voters' first preferences. So under the alternative vote, some second preferences (those which are second preferences behind a first preference for a candidate who is to be eliminated) get 'promoted' into first preferences, and other second preferences are not reviewed. Under STV's procedure for distributing 'surplus' votes, a proportion of the second preferences of all persons voting for a successful candidate are added to the total for other candidates, a total previously given by the number of first preferences expressed for them. Finally, no system can be said to allow for equal counting of equal preferences if the equality of preference refers to the intensity, rather than rank, of that preference.

Does each voter equally contribute to determining the outcome? Once again we must remember we have already put aside the idea of potential equality, that before the vote is taken each person may be said to have an equal influence on the result. The question we are now considering is concerned with the 'backward-looking' question: given the way that votes were cast, and the result of the aggregation procedure, did all votes equally contribute to determining the outcome? This is where the accusation about 'wasted' votes is normally levelled at the plurality system, first because a candidate may be elected by a majority far in excess of what is required, and secondly because the votes of those who voted for unsuccessful candidates (even when the winning majority is tiny) play no further role in the election.

The important consideration here, of course, is the notion of the outcome. If we restrict our idea of the outcome to the result in a particular constituency employing the plurality system, then it could be claimed that, even retrospectively, all votes contributed equally to determine the result. Each was counted, and each counted for one. But this is not the relevant sense of the outcome which supporters of rival PR systems have in mind. That sense of the outcome is wider. It refers not to the selection of a particular person, but to the relationship between all the ballots cast and all the persons elected, and to the composition of the representative assembly produced by putting together the results in all the different constituencies. The quota system in STV, for example, might be said to keep in play as many preferences as possible for as long as possible, so that some part of everyone's preference ordering contributes to the overall outcome.

What is the balance between the choice of an individual voter and a party's choice?

When we were discussing the amount of preference information an individual was allowed to express, we pointed out that the ability to write-in the name of a candidate is an extension of the voters' choice. We have also recognized the importance of the parties' role in the nomination procedure that produces the names on the ballot paper, even under a plurality system. Clearly the same questions about the openness of the nomination procedure can be asked of any electoral mechanism. Party list systems introduce the new consideration of any party's ranking of its candidates, over which, at the extreme, the individual voter has no control. One might think of a spectrum running between total voter choice (any individual voter can vote for anyone) to strict party listing (in which the voter has no control over which individual receives his or her vote). We should remember that party list systems occupy a fair range of the end of this spectrum, giving variable degrees of voter choice, as Urwin's example of the Swiss case was designed to bring out.

The search for a 'best' system

The search for a voting system which can be agreed to be 'the best' faces a number of difficulties. First, as we have already seen, there can be no ideal system, and further points are made about this below. Secondly, even when we move to the search for the best system we can achieve in given circumstances, there remain two sources of likely controversy. The first is the criteria by which an electoral system should be assessed. Even restricting ourselves to criteria drawn from democratic theory, we may find different understandings of what the requirements of democracy are, or how they are to be understood. For example, there is no agreement as to whether strategic voting should be treated as a hazard to democratic practice, something to be minimized, or whether it is a necessary and even valuable part of that practice. The second source of difficulty, once we have an agreed set of criteria by which to make the assessment, is that a voting system which does well by one test (say, of simplicity and cheapness) may do badly by another (say, of taking all preferences into account). There then arises the problem of making an assessment 'on balance'.

One way of demonstrating that there is no ideal voting system is due to Arrow, who showed that there are formal limits to the capacity of any electoral system, since it is a system of preference aggregation, to take all the preference information into account and yet produce a determinate, fair, and collectively rational result.[7] This is simply an informal way of stating Arrow's theorem. That theorem proved that no voting system can satisfy four conditions which seem very desirable requirements of any voting system with a claim to be democratic. These conditions are, first, the requirement that if all voters rank one outcome above another, then the aggregation of their preferences should also rank that outcome above the other. The second condition is the condition of non-dictatorship. This requires that there is no voter whose preference for one outcome over another is always able to determine that the collective ordering will correspond to his or her ranking with respect to those outcomes. The third condition is completeness: that there should be a collective preference ordering for all preferences that voters could possibly hold. Finally, Arrow's last condition was the 'independence of irrelevant alternatives'. This requires that if two outcomes are being compared, their ranking should depend only on those two outcomes, and therefore it should not be affected by the introduction of other possibilities. Colman provides an amusing illustration of the apparent irrationality of violating the condition of the irrelevance of independent alternatives. A diner looks at the menu, from which he understands he has a choice between salmon and steak. He orders salmon, but then the waiter informs him that chicken is also available today. 'In that case,' says the diner, 'I'll take the steak.' By reversing his preference between salmon and steak after the irrelevant alternative of chicken has been offered, the diner appears to be acting irrationally (Colman 1982: 28).

Arrow's theorem proved that no voting system could satisfy these four conditions. He was able to demonstrate that the Condorcet paradox discussed earlier is simply a special case of the problem. Clearly, his finding places theoretical limits on what can be achieved by any system of preference aggregation, and since electoral systems are systems which aggregate voters' preferences, it applies to them. But dramatic though Arrow's theorem is, it is important to be clear about its significance. It is a proof that no voting system can guarantee to meet the stated conditions, given the logically possible preference orderings of the voters. This by itself says nothing about the probability that the logically possible preference orderings which will lead to the non-fulfilment of the conditions are ones actually held by voters. So a good deal of work has gone into the investigation of the properties of voting systems when likely rather than logically possible preferences are taken in view (Sugden 1981: 156).

A second consideration common to all voting systems is their vulnerability to strategic voting. If strategic voting is considered to be undesirable, then part of the assessment of alternative electoral systems will be the degree of this vulnerability, that is the ease with which it can be practised. Those who oppose strategic voting appear to have three concerns, which we may characterize as focusing on honesty, fairness, and accuracy respectively.

The first, and general, objection is that strategic voting is dishonest, since it involves the misrepresentation of the voter's true preferences. For example, rather than voting honestly for candidate A, the voter claims to prefer B in order to keep out C whom he least favours, and whom he suspects has a good chance of winning. We have already dismissed the claim that the voter's strategic preferences are in some way not his or her true preferences. The argument against strategic voting may survive that dismissal if the claim is that voting should not be regarded instrumentally, but should rather be treated demonstratively. The voter should, on this view, demonstrate publicly whom he or she finds worthy of support, rather than treat the vote as an instrument to achieve his or her highest preferences given the preferences of others. Such an argument need not suppose that this instrumentality aims to pursue narrow self-interest: altruistic voters may well make strategic calculations. Nevertheless, it suggests that there is some virtue in stating one's true preferences, even if they are ineffective, and even if the opportunity cost is the selection of the alternative which, from this voter's point of view, is the worst one.

The second argument against strategic voting may appear to derive from a concern with honesty, but in fact relies on a notion of fairness. Someone who misrepresents his or her preferences *when others vote sincerely* appears to be taking unfair advantage of their sincerity. But this is only an unfair advantage if they do not have the same opportunity to vote strategically as he or she does. This opportunity will be unequally distributed if (1) some voters do not understand the voting system as fully as others and/or (2) some voters have better information about the intentions of the rest of the electorate than others.[8] If other voters have an equal opportunity to vote strategically, yet decline to do so on ethical grounds, then the strategic voter is certainly taking advantage of their ethical stance, but is not doing so unfairly.

The third argument worries about the aggregation procedure. Is it not possible if a large number of people vote strategically that the result will in some sense be worse, in aggregate, than if they had all voted sincerely? These strategic voters must base their strategy, if voting is simultaneous or secret, on their expectations of how others will vote, and these expectations may be incorrect. Indeed, they may be wrong because others have deliberately tried to give a misleading impression of their intentions, in order to increase their chances of securing a desired result. Is it not possible that in this world of individual voters trying to outguess each other, at as many levels of complexity as we care to consider, that their misjudgements will lead to a situation which is worse, in aggregate, than if they were all sincere voters?

Let us consider a simple example of five voters, three candidates and plurality voting.

V	W	X	Y	Z
A	B	B	A	B
B	C	A	B	C
C	A	C	C	A

Sincere voting will lead to the choice of *B*. Suppose *V* and *Y* recognize this. To get *A* elected they need to obtain one more vote for *A* from *W*, *X* or *Z*. *A* is *W*'s and *Z*'s last choice; but *X* has *A* in second place over *C*. *V* and *Y* might truly believe that *W* and *Z* plan to vote for *C*, perhaps because *W* and *Z* have said they will as part of their strategy, or they might believe that *W* and *Z* plan to vote for *B* but mislead *X* so *X* believes that they plan to vote for C. If X thought that his or her vote would be determinate between A and C, his or her strategic vote would go to A. A would then be elected, if others vote sincerely, despite (1) only two 'original' first preferences; (2) only one second preference; and (3) two last preferences. It looks plausible to suppose that the more outguessing that goes on, the more likely that the aggregate outcome will be worse than that achieved by sincere voting.

But this depends on their being an unambiguous sense of the outcome being 'worse in aggregate', and the example just given is rather misleading. It is misleading in two ways. First, it runs together the idea that a voter can be mistaken about the voting intentions of other voters with the idea that a voter can be deliberately misled about those intentions by those who stand to benefit from spreading the false information. Clearly no-one can devise a voting system which will eliminate either possibility, but the objection to manipulating other voters is an objection to the practice of manipulation, not to the voting system which 'allows' it to occur.[9] The *opportunity* to vote strategically derives from the fact that voters have a schedule of preferences, not simply a most preferred choice. The *incentive* to vote strategically arises from expectations about how others will vote. But this is true whether or not the information any voter has is accurate. If every voter had perfect knowledge of the sincere preferences of every other voter, he or she would still have to decide whether others, knowing what they know, will vote sincerely or strategically. One sense in which the outcome might be 'better on aggregate' if there were no strategic voting is that a voter not taking account of how others are expected to vote cannot get it wrong, and will not be working on false information; but, then, we rule out the opportunity to get it right as well.

The second sense in which the example is rather misleading is that it runs together the notion that multiple levels of strategic voting lead to an indeterminate answer with the idea that the result is in some way worse. But, as Condorcet's paradox shows, a determinate answer need not be the best or the right answer: it simply is the answer. One problem is that different voting systems return different answers when the 'raw material' of preferences is aggregated, as was illustrated earlier. Another problem is that voting systems provide an opportunity and an incentive to vote strategically, which means that the 'raw material' of expressed preferences is not fixed. This lack of fixity may lead to an indeterminate answer in the sense that we do not know what the best outcome would be; but since the votes are taken at a particular time, there will be an answer.

This all leads to the conclusion that the disputed status of strategic voting should lead us to concentrate on the question of fairness. We have argued that no voting system can eliminate the opportunity and incentive to vote strategically, and that the important argument from fairness requires that all voters have the same opportunity to collect information about both the voting system and the intentions of others. This reinforces a conclusion we drew from the example of the voting system employed in the Channel Islands legislature,[10] that the electoral system should deprive voters of knowledge of how others have in fact voted until everyone has done so. Another dispute about electoral practice to which it relates concerns the publication of opinion polls. It has been suggested that eve-of-poll tests of public opinion are undesirable, because they have an effect on voters' intentions and therefore interfere with the democratic process. Our argument does not lead to any conclusion about a desirable cut-off point for the publication of such information; but it does suggest that it should be equally available to everyone.

It is also important to remember the point made about Arrow's theorem: it demonstrates that no voting system can meet the four conditions for every theoretically feasible set of voters' preferences, irrespective of whether these are likely or even plausible preferences for anyone to hold. A similar point can be made about strategic voting. There is no voting system which is immune to it, in the sense that there is no voting system which does not allow a voter the opportunity and the incentive to vote strategically given particular patterns of preference. But in practice the opportunity and the incentive are stronger under some systems than others, especially when we take account of the different senses of the 'outcome' of an election which we have identified, as a comparison between plurality voting and STV makes clear.

Since a plurality winner takes all at the constituency level, every voter needs to be concerned with 'limiting the damage' (measured by reference to his or her sincere preference schedule) of that outcome. The only reason to vote for a candidate who is not going to take all would be the demonstrative value of the act; but such a 'losing' preference plays no further part in the outcome of the election at either the constituency or the Parliamentary level. (Equally, of course, there is no incentive, other than a demonstrative one, to vote for a candidate who is expected to win anyway – at least if the voter assumes that other voters will not free-ride as well.[11]) If the expectation is that the first-preference candidate has no chance, then the objective is to try to obtain the next highest possible preference. The predictions that a first-preference candidate has no chance and that a second-preference candidate might have require very little knowledge. Under STV, by contrast, the outcome of the election at both constituency and Parliamentary level (assuming STV with multiple constituencies) is affected by voters' preference orderings, and information required to vote strategically is much more complex.

A rather different limitation of electoral systems concerns their ability to achieve proportionality between votes cast and seats allocated. Clearly, different electoral systems are likely to yield different results in terms of the correspondence between the share of the votes a party obtains, and its share of the seats. Although in everyday political debate it is usual to draw a simple distinction between proportional and non-proportional systems of voting, in fact there is considerable variation in the effects of different forms of PR. For example, by comparison with many other PR systems, the d'Hondt formula mentioned earlier allocates seats to parties in such a way that small parties are usually penalized. Generally, those polities using PR are more proportional in their allocation of seats to parties than those politics which employ non-PR systems.[12] However, the PR systems employed in some countries, such as Spain, seem to produce allocations of seats which are less proportional than allocations in some of the countries which do not use PR (Gunther 1989).

CONCLUSION

We have reviewed the consequences of two theoretical limitations on all democratic voting systems: that proposed by Arrow, and vulnerability to strategic voting (which follows from it). We may now turn to a suggested solution to the dilemma of choosing an electoral system. The dilemma is by now obvious. We know that voting systems have different properties, and we know that existing political parties and voters have particular views about the voting system under which they expect to do well (however they interpret that). How could there be an impartial decision about the best system to adopt? Any proposal to decide by using a voting system will suffer from an infinite regress, while if we leave the decision to the political market place we simply reinforce the existing pattern of advantage.

The search for a neutral procedure has been a common liberal ambition. If only the procedure is neutral, the hope is, then the result will be acceptable. This holds for fair trials, for the neutrality of the state, and for ideas about justice. By analogy, the best voting system is one chosen impartially, and the best result in an election is the result which follows from the use of a fair electoral system. So, building on work done in the tradition of the social contract, and more particularly on Rawls' contractarian theory of justice,[13] it could be suggested that a fair voting system is one which we would agree to use, in ignorance of our own political preferences and those of other citizens. Each of us would then have to be concerned not only with the hope that we could prosper as part of a majority, but also with the dangers of not flourishing because we were in a minority. The consequences of this may be informally elaborated.

The condition of ignorance (about the pattern of preferences, including our own) makes our choice of a voting system a decision under uncertainty. If we knew what numbers to attach to particular opinion blocs in society, we could calculate the chances of being in a majority, and decide according to our attitudes to risk. For example, if I thought there was a good chance that I would be in the majority, I might well favour a winner-takes-all system, in the same way as (the bulk) of the Conservative and Labour parties. But in the hypothetical contract we do not have that knowledge. Moreover, we have to recognize that both our own opinions, and those of other voters, may change over time. The basis on which a rational decision should be made in conditions of such uncertainty is still unsettled, but it seems plausible to suppose that a self-interested concern to do as well as possible for oneself will focus on minimizing the damage if one turns out to be in a minority. More formally, each person will want to minimize the regret he or she feels when his or her preferences are revealed after the decision rule has been chosen. So, for all the possible electoral systems, each person has to consider how much he or she would regret the choice of that voting system, given the preferences he or she might turn out to hold in relation to everyone else. This amounts to saying that each voter will want the electoral system which gives him or her the greatest influence, even if that voter's opinions are shared by very few others.

At the same time, such a voter would be concerned with the stability of the political system. It is a popular argument that PR tends to fragment a party system, and that in turn this makes governing more difficult. If this argument were correct, then the more proportional an electoral system was, the greater the danger of instability in the regime. In fact, there are a number of other considerations which are crucial in determining whether instability is likely to occur. Nevertheless, we can point to real-world examples in which highly proportional electoral systems have facilitated the proliferation of small parties and rendered government more difficult. An obvious example is Israel. In choosing an electoral system, then, the voter would weigh up the possible adverse effects of maximizing the influence of minority parties, of which he or she might be a supporter, against the expected benefits.

We have suggested that the voter choosing an electoral system under conditions of uncertainty will seek the greatest influence for minorities, compatible with the desired level of stable government. But 'greatest influence' in the context of an electoral system refers not only to the composition of the representative assembly, but also to the formation of government, as we saw in Chapter 4.[14] It would be impossible to choose an electoral system to achieve this aim without knowing the conventions surrounding government formation. For example, in Canada, and arguably in Britain, where there are many fewer historical instances, there is a preference among the major parties to opt for minority government, rather than for coalition government formation, when no party has an overall Parliamentary majority. This preference, however, seems to reflect the fact that the absence of a working Parliamentary majority is fairly uncommon – and the situation is not likely to last beyond the next election. It cannot be assumed that the parties would continue to behave in this way if they expected the lack of a working Parliamentary majority to be a regular occurrence. Obviously, it is impossible to predict the new conventions about government formation that might arise. For this reason, voters trying to choose an electoral system seem necessarily to be denied the sort of information they need.

The 'minimax' approach to choosing an electoral system provides no solutions – it is simply a specification of the requirements of fairness. Once we recognize that fairness is only one of the values we seek to achieve, we must also acknowledge that 'trade-offs' between those values will be made in different ways by different people. Additionally, as we have just seen, there are unlikely to be common assumptions about the political practices that could emerge in the wake of alternative electoral systems. Much of the debate between those who defend the present British electoral system and those who oppose it derives from differing weights being attached to the value of fairness, and from differing predictions about the content of possible new conventions relating to government formation. It is not surprising, therefore, that advocates in these debates tend to 'talk past each other': they do not realize that they could agree about the properties of electoral systems, and yet conscientiously disagree about these other matters.

8   Conclusion

Throughout this study, we have been concerned to explore the British electoral system by drawing upon different approaches to the study of politics and by looking for revealing contrasts and comparisons. Since these comparisons are of various kinds, it will be helpful, in concluding, to draw them together, and a number of the most important ones will be reviewed in the next section. In the second section we briefly note the advantages and limitations of the different perspectives we have adopted, and finally we explain why the subject of our enquiry requires the integration of these approaches.

COMPARATIVE PERSPECTIVES

The major objective of any discipline is to stand back from the object of study and to subject it to much greater scrutiny than it would otherwise receive. This can sometimes be true in a very literal sense: the powerful radio telescopes of astronomers allow the universe to be scrutinized in ways which are not available to more casual observers, no matter how keen their interest in the stars. In relation to political practice, the analyst strives to obtain both greater depth and greater breadth than either the casual observer or the participant, and this insight is sought, in the study of politics as elsewhere, by continually asking the question, why? But in relation to a social practice, like that of electing representatives or leaders, this question is a twofold one. It is asking not only for an explanation of why events occur as they do, or why a particular procedure has, as a matter of fact, been adopted, but also for justification: since our institutions are (to an extent which may be disputed) under our control and of our own making, what is the justification for our adopting this practice rather than that? This concern with justification is necessarily a concern with our values. And, of course, our awareness of alternatives, our knowledge of how they operate, is dependent upon precisely the breadth mentioned just now. It is only if we enquire how matters are arranged in systems other than our own, or how they have been arranged in our own system in the past, or what suggestions have been made about preferable alternative arrangements, that we can either know our range of choice or be equipped with the information which will support our justifications.

All this is fairly commonplace, but it explains our concern in this study to draw on a variety of approaches to the study of politics, and to extend the range of informative comparison as far as possible. This obviously involves examining what might otherwise be taken for granted, and pushing on with the question, why? At the most basic level, we do not want to assume that the current British electoral system has always been in use in the United Kingdom, nor do we want to assume that there is something natural and inevitable about it. Nor do we want to leave unexamined the notion that democracy is a matter of 'one person, one vote', either historically or analytically. Our most general theme has been that electoral systems are a matter of choice, and that this choice requires justification. We have sustained that case by trying to draw attention to a range of relevant comparisons, of which the following are the most important.

Elections as decision-making devices

The two issues which involve both classification and comparison here are, first, what is an election, and secondly, when is it appropriate to use elections as a means to arrive at a decision? In the political context, but not in all contexts in which elections are employed, the usual purpose of elections is to choose particular individuals who will take decisions. The process of election may be contrasted with other methods of arranging for an outcome which will be applied to a group, such as direct democracy, and this raises an issue which has recurred throughout our study: what is the relation between electoral systems and democratic practice? We also saw that democracy can be seen as one of a group of six methods of arriving at a decision, and it is important to recognize that these six methods can be used in combination. Voting is an integral part of democracy, and, except under a wholly direct democracy, elections of decision-makers are required as a substitute for voting on all decisions. In this way, elections may be combined with authoritative determination and with chance. This is one of the reasons we have for supposing that electoral systems may be required to fulfil many different tasks simultaneously.

Comparison through time

Our present electoral practice has a history, and we usually expect to be able to understand such a practice more easily if we have some idea of its development. Historical comparison can not only reveal alternative practices which have been employed in the past, but also disclose the reasons for which that practice changed. Perhaps three of the historical variations are particularly important: the extent of the electorate, in relation to sex, age and property qualifications; the extent to which multiple votes and multiple representation has occurred; and the grafting of the idea of personal representation on to the earlier notion of territorial representation. To some extent these changes reflect new understandings of the requirements of democracy, particularly the view that true democracy requires not merely an extensive franchise but a universal one.

Personal and territorial representation

It is plain that the existing electoral system in Britain has emerged from an earlier system which aimed to achieve the representation of territorial units. Clearly, we can compare an electoral system which aims to represent persons with one which aims to represent territory. But since the actual system presently in use has grafted one aim upon the other, we once again find that elections as a device to choose decision-makers are also burdened with multiple roles in achieving represent-ation. An additional level of complexity arises from the connection between representation and democracy. The problem of the form of representation which is 'most democratic' becomes a problem about how an electoral system should be structured to secure that represent-ation. When more than one kind of representation is aimed at – both personal and territorial, for example – it is likely, once again, that neither task will be achieved as fully as would be possible if one form of representation were aimed at exclusively.

Direct and indirect democracy

The difference between direct democracy, in which individuals collectively regulate their affairs by sharing decisions which will be applied to the group as a whole, and indirect democracy, in which individuals choose others who will make those decisions, obviously explains the need for a mechanism to choose the decision-makers. One such mechanism is an electoral system. But criteria derived from the practice of direct democracy can be used to assess the extent of democracy in an indirect system which employs elections. For example, for those who value democracy because it involves political participation and political equality, some obvious questions to ask of an electoral system are: do all persons affected by the decision-makers have equal resources to deploy in selecting them? How wide is the franchise? How frequent are elections? But in addition to this notion that indirect democracy can achieve the objectives of direct democracy in a modified or truncated form, it is sometimes suggested that elections can reveal 'the will of the people' or 'the general will'. Hence the result of an election is treated as if it were comparable to the outcome of the voting in a genuine popular assembly. Once again, elections are asked to do too many jobs: an electoral system employs a voting system, but this does not mean that an electoral system can fulfil the aims of a voting system in a direct democracy.

Voting systems and electoral systems

When committee members vote on a resolution which is under discussion, their votes are counted in favour or against adopting the proposal being debated. There is a direct connection between individual members' votes and the policy outcome. When individuals vote to elect representatives who then vote on the policies, the connection is much less direct. The crucial difference in the present context is how the electors' votes are to be interpreted. There are two problems of interpretation to consider here.

First, voting systems are vulnerable to strategic voting. This means that even in the relatively simple case of the committee members, we cannot straightforwardly infer that a vote for or against a proposal tells us the attitude of the voter to that issue if it were taken singly and if the committee member were voting in complete ignorance of other members' attitudes. If many issues are decided together, it may pay members to trade votes on issues they are relatively indifferent about for votes on issues they care deeply about: they will vote differently from how they would have done if one issue alone were determined. (Of course, any decision-making system which persists through time raises the prospect of vote trading, provided someone is prepared to change his or her vote and trusts someone else to do the same when the favour is called in, on a yet unknown issue. But it is especially likely to arise when an agenda contains a large number of known issues which are decided together, either within one resolution or within one session of a committee.) Vote trading and strategic voting require knowledge of

others' voting intentions: voting on a committee for my second-preference outcome, in order to ensure that my last-preference outcome does
not defeat my first-preference outcome, obviously requires information
about how others are likely to vote. For these reasons, even in the
'simple' case of a committee, we should be careful how we interpret votes.
Votes in favour or against a proposal may be sincere votes, truly
expressing an individual's attitude to the proposal in isolation from
other issues and from the attitudes of other committee members; but
they may also be, and indeed they are more likely to be, votes influenced
by the strategic structure of the situation. This problem of 'interpreting'
a vote applies equally to the use of a voting system by a committee
determining policy, and to the votes of electors choosing representatives.

But a second problem of interpretation arises only in electoral
systems. Under the present plurality system, any individual's vote may
be treated as expressing support for a whole range of outcomes
associated with that system. That is, a vote for Leftwing could be
'interpreted' to include at least these: (1) expressing the view that
Leftwing is the best MP for my constituency (remembering that 'best'
could mean 'best for me' or 'best for us'); (2) a vote in favour of
Leftwing's party (because or despite of Leftwing herself); (3) a vote in
favour of the policies apparently espoused by Leftwing's party
(remembering the problem of full-line supply); (4) an expression of the
opinion that the leader of Leftwing's party would make the 'best' Prime
Minister on offer. But unless we know the intentions of the individual
voter, we do not know which of these meanings to impute to his or her
vote. The possible imputations run together aspects of direct democracy
– attitudes to policies – with the mechanisms of indirect democracy – the
selection of leaders and representatives.

The possible range of interpretations depends upon the electoral
system in use. Clearly, a strict party list system rules out the prospect of
a vote being interpreted as support for a particular candidate, because
there is no provision under that system for a voter to endorse individuals
rather than parties. But although the range of possible interpretations
may vary, there will still be multiple possibilities. This problem, unlike
that of strategic voting, is a problem of electoral systems rather than
voting systems as such. It is a key part of our argument that elections are
liable to be overburdened as political devices.

British practice and that of other systems

Since the focus of this book is electoral systems in Britain, we have
introduced examples drawn from other systems to illuminate or comment

upon particular features of the British case. We have not been involved in a sustained comparative study of the electoral systems currently in use, which would require a different sort of book. The points of comparison and contrast we have noted, nonetheless, are important, and lead to a question about how 'divisible' the electoral system, in a broad sense, actually is. The question arises in this way.

We have established that the plurality system currently employed in Britain is empirically rare: very few liberal democratic polities in the contemporary world employ it. If we ask what the consequences are of particular systems of election, we encounter a problem. We need to know whether other observable differences between British political practice, and that of the systems being used in a comparison, have independent explanations – they have nothing to do with the system of election – or whether they are in some way causally linked to that system. If they are causally linked, these other aspects cannot be divorced from the electoral system itself, and should become part of the package of comparison. It is this problem, for example, which lies behind some of the dispute about the desirability of electoral reform.

Is a plurality voting system linked to strong and stable government? Does proportional representation necessarily require coalition government, or give rise to a weak regime? If the connections *were* well-established, the basis of comparison (and, indeed, choice) should be a package which takes the connections into account: plurality voting and strong government versus proportional representation and weak coalition government. In fact, of course, these particular examples cannot be sustained: the connections are not well established. But other cases present more plausible relations between the electoral system narrowly defined and the rest of the polity. Plurality voting is biased against small, new and dispersed parties; proportional representation may encourage a proliferation of parties. In a nutshell, the problem of comparison is how 'divisible' political practice is: can we sensibly imagine replacing plurality voting with proportional voting and continuing with existing conventions about government formation, or are those conventions and the electoral system an indivisible unit?

Comparisons of properties of electoral systems

We have compared the properties of two classes of electoral systems: those actually in use, a comparison which leads to the problem just discussed, and those which have been put forward as desirable, even though they are not presently employed in national elections, such as the Borda Count. Clearly, assessing the merits of a proposed voting system when we cannot observe the apparent consequences of its use in an existing political system raises peculiar difficulties, and perhaps this explains why much of the study of voting systems has focused on the abstract mathematical exploration of their properties.

We have also made rather more specific comparisons within the range of electoral systems thus identified. We have met the conventional distinction between majoritarian and proportional voting systems, and we have also compared specific voting systems one with another. For example, we have looked at the Alternative Vote in comparison with STV. Part of the objective here is to address the problem mentioned above: to what extent is the electoral system 'divisible'? Comparing polities which employ different electoral systems should draw our attention to other differences which can be causally connected to the primary difference in the system of voting. Moreover, since there is an indefinite number of possible electoral systems, the point of examining well-known variants comparatively is not merely to consider arguments about the superiority of one over another, but also to isolate the various 'building blocks' or aspects of the voting system about which we can make choices: for example, how many votes should each elector have available? Should the elector be able to endorse a candidate, a party, or both?

THE VALUE OF DIFFERENT APPROACHES

We have also been concerned with the utility of different approaches to the study of the British electoral system, believing that the various approaches all have something to offer in a full understanding of contemporary practice. But, of course, it is the integration of the various perspectives which is important. There are two points here. First, the approaches are in some ways complementary: one can supply insights denied to another. Secondly, the integration of approaches is demanded by the nature of the topic. Both points may be pursued by looking at the 'approaches' in question.

Historical study

The great benefit of the historical study of the British electoral system is its concreteness. It is possible to provide a picture of the major developments as they occurred. Such historical study, we have already noticed, draws attention to features which are too easily overlooked by an exclusive concentration on contemporary practice. But the range of comparison it can encompass is at the same time limited by the historical experience described. Since the United Kingdom has never employed STV in Parliamentary elections (with the exception of some of the university seats between 1918 and 1945), for example, an examination of historical experience will not draw it to our attention; on the other hand, we shall be alerted to the importance of the extent of the franchise and the difference between personal and territorial representation. But the history of one electoral system which has not undergone very radical change can obviously provide only a limited amount of suggestive experience.

Public choice theory

Theories of social choice are not constrained to examine only those voting systems which have been used. Because of the use of models, such theories can look at possible as well as actual voting systems. The most important characteristic of public choice theory, for present purposes, is that it offers simplified models of complex political situations. Clearly, this is both a strength and a weakness: while we cannot have the concreteness of historical or contemporary empirical study, we can hope that the assumptions of the model are such as to give it general applicability. Such models have to be constructed with sufficient detail to have some purchase on a complex world, but with sufficient economy to be truly simplifying. We have employed the findings of public choice theory in a number of ways. In our examination of the appropriateness of elections as decision-making devices, we examined alternatives with the insights of public choice theory. In our examination of voting systems, and in particular of the limitations of aggregating votes, we drew on theories of social choice. We have also looked at some problems from the point of view of the rational political actor who is a key figure in public choice models, as in our consideration of strategic voting and the secrecy of elections. We have to bear constantly in mind, however, that public choice models, when properly constructed, aim to make clear the consequences of a restricted set of assumptions. Hence such reasoning can tell us, to put an example informally, that if political actors are rational, if they have particular sets of preferences, if they have knowledge of one another's preferences, then strategic voting will occur. Similarly, we can provide a deductive model to explain the occurrence of logrolling. Again, mathematical proof can be provided that no voting system is immune to strategic voting. But none of this tells us just how much strategic voting actually goes on in any particular voting system, and public choice models are neither designed nor equipped to do so.

Political science

In a broad sense, of course, all the approaches mentioned here form part of 'political science'. But, more narrowly, we here use the term to refer to the findings of comparative political enquiry – such as the thesis that voting systems actually in use in countries studied have an impact on the party system and upon the electoral tactics of political parties – and to the typologies with which such analysis is associated. Hence classifications of electoral systems, and notions like the 'phases' of those systems, provide helpful ways of thinking about the elements of electoral systems and the political features apparently associated with them. A view persists that this sort of descriptive (and, more ambitiously, explanatory) endeavour can be divorced from normative considerations. Even if this were well founded, for anyone who is primarily concerned with electoral systems because of their connection with democracy such typologies (and explanations of causal links) provide only the raw material for argument about the major concern. While we have drawn upon and assessed such classifications and explanations, in previous chapters, we have also wanted to explore the connections between electoral systems and democratic theory.

Normative political theory

Normative political theory is concerned with the explication and rational justification of values invoked in the course of political activity. Political theory thus conceived certainly has a long history, and it is perfectly legitimate to deploy arguments put within that tradition in the assessment of contemporary arrangements, provided adequate attention is given to changes in the context of argument. Hence John Stuart Mill's discussion of the benefits of open voting is still important, as long as we are sensitive to the many ways in which the polity of the 1990s differs from that of the 1860s. Additionally, we have prescriptive arguments about the benefits of particular arrangements, even when these have never been realized. This raises a question about the relationship between normative argument – for example, about the value of high levels of participation, or about the pursuit of political equality – and the findings of political science, a question which has generated a great deal of discussion and controversy in its application to democratic theory, so we may conclude by focusing on our conception of how the approaches mentioned fit together in the exposition of this essay.

CHOOSING AN ELECTORAL SYSTEM

Electoral systems are a matter for choice. There is an indefinite number of possible systems, and many elements for decision. For example, what threshold of votes should be set for the allocation of seats in a proportional system – 5 per cent, 10 per cent? Such a decision is a simple illustration of what is at stake in the wider choice we are discussing. But before we go further in exploring the nature of this choice, there is a preliminary consideration to clear away.

We can imagine (as we did in considering the 'ideal' voting system) that we are choosing an electoral system for a polity which has yet to be brought into being. Alternatively, we can look at the existing practice in a polity like Britain, and ask whether we think it can be improved by reform. As we have already noticed, providing answers to these questions requires rather different approaches: the one is best tackled as a problem in rational choice, while the other requires sensitivity and judgement about the nature of the polity to be 'reformed'. The two questions differ in another fundamental way. If we ask, in the abstract, what electoral system is most to be preferred, imagining that we are about to set it up *de novo*, we do not have to take account of the costs of change. If, however, we contemplate reform of existing practice, such costs have to be taken into consideration: we might feel they outweigh the benefits of reform. One such cost is particularly germane, and it was discussed earlier in this essay. If the electoral system is consistently manipulated for partisan advantage by existing power-holders, the 'neutrality' of the electoral system (which is, of course, technically a variable) is threatened. Whatever our views about the nature of the desirable electoral system, the risk that whatever degree of neutrality it can achieve is undermined needs to be taken into account, even if we decide it is a risk worth taking. Of course, the alternative view is that reform would require a consensus on desirable change, which will never emerge if the interests of existing power-holders are at stake. Our preliminary point about the nature of choice is simply a recognition that, when we speak of reform, there is a *status quo*, but when we abstract behind a veil of ignorance there is not.

Even if this means that there are costs to be entered on the balance sheet, it does not deny that the electoral system is one which we choose. And if an institution is chosen, and capable of modification, the obvious implication is that we should be able to justify whatever choice we make. Questions of justification might seem immediately to require the sort of normative argument which has been discussed above. But it is equally true that such justification requires the insights of history, political science, and public choice theory. This is because justifications have to be couched in terms of the institutional consequences, assessed in terms of our values, of particular electoral systems. And any claim about the institutional consequences of such systems (for example, the effect on the party system, or the degree of proportionality achieved) is first and foremost a claim which can be sustained only by reference to empirical material (gleaned from historical example or comparative study), or to the properties of electoral systems (gleaned from theories of social choice). The impact of these institutional effects on our values (once we have elucidated them – for example, how exactly we understand the requirements of democracy) is a second question, even if it is this one which we happen to think is the most important.

All this means that there can be no question of dividing the empirical from the normative: when we want to justify a political practice, we have to integrate these concerns. And it is of course true that this gives us a diagnosis of conscientious disagreement about what the most desirable electoral system is. On the one hand, there is undoubtedly 'scientific' disagreement about the relation of the alleged institutional conse-quences of the electoral system – there is no consensus about the precise degree of influence it has on party systems, for example. On the other hand, there is normative disagreement, not only about the proper understanding of terms like 'democracy', but also about the impact of the institutional consequences, even if agreed, upon those values. For example, we might agree that a particular electoral system is associated with coalition government, but disagree about the impact of conven-tions governing coalition formation, and the negotiation of coalition policies, on the democratic character of the polity. It is clear, though, that rational debate will necessitate drawing upon the complementary approaches which we have just reviewed; and that rational disagreement about 'what should be done' is entirely possible. Hence the two authors of this essay differ in their preferences for reform, while trusting that their own preferences are not known to the reader.

Notes

1 INTRODUCTION

1 'Electoral Laws are those which govern the processes by which electoral preferences are articulated as votes and by which these votes are translated into distributions of governmental authority (typically parliamentary seats) among the competing political parties' (Rae 1971: 14).
2 For a useful introduction to the political relevance of some of the ideas, see McLean (1987).
3 A similar view is found in Canada, where third parties have captured (between them) at least 20 per cent of the total vote since 1958 and have obtained a greater share of Parliamentary seats than in Britain. But debate about electoral reform for federal elections in Canada has been even more muted than in Britain – except in the context of reducing regional imbalances in the parties' representation in Parliament.
4 Polling is problematic for two reasons. There is a problem of the connection between what people say, hypothetically, they would do and what they would actually do in the polling booth. Moreover, individuals may even deliberately misreport what they have done when voting, so that under some circumstances there may be a large number of 'lying' voters. For example, exit polls taken at the 1989 elections in Virginia and New York City indicated that the black Democratic candidates for Governor and Mayor respectively would win quite easily. In fact, while these polls predicted accurately the results of other elections held at the same time, they greatly exaggerated the margin of victory of these two candidates. The widely accepted explanation of this is that many voters did not wish to admit publicly that they had let racial considerations determine their vote and so they lied to the poll-takers.

2 WHAT IS AN ELECTION?

1 For a discussion of the important role of 'organized chance' in securing social justice see Goodwin (1984).
2 One of the most common types of game requiring a mixed strategy are games without saddle points. For a full explanation see Colman (1982: Chapter 4). In such games the best strategy for a player will depend on what other people choose to do, but since they must make their moves simultaneously they all

try to 'second guess' what the others will do. In order to conceal his intentions, a player should utilize decision-making procedures which incorporate chance elements.

3 The question of how the membership of such groups is to be identified is one to which we return in the third section.

4 The case of so-called 'recall elections' in which voters are asked whether they wish to remove an elected official from office prematurely, might appear to weaken the distinction between a referendum and an election. But 'a recall election' does not fit the definition of an election quoted earlier; it is a referendum because it takes a policy decision rather than selecting an officeholder.

5 It should be pointed out that the theory of voting was invented in the eighteenth century (by Condorcet and Borda) and reinvented in the nineteenth century (by Lewis Carroll) to deal with these sorts of electoral problems, and not in the context of selecting representatives.

6 There have been instances, though, of individuals giving up the papacy, such as Celestine V.

7 On the free-riding problem, see Olson (1965).

8 We are grateful to Jeff Stanyer for providing us with the details of this case.

9 In fact, there is no direct correspondence between voting strength and power. A full discussion of these, and related, issues is provided by Barry (1980).

10 From 1918 until 1928 only women over thirty were entitled to vote. More generally, reducing the qualifying age for the vote brings the following two groups into closer correspondence – those entitled to vote, and those affected by the decision-making process. In Britain the present threshold of eighteen years was established in 1970, having previously been twenty-one.

11 The idea was first introduced in a formal way by a political scientist in Friedrich (1937: 16–18).

12 The idea of a mandate is explained in detail in the subsection 'Representation and the election of governments' in Chapter 4.

13 A natural monopoly is one in which the marginal cost of supply is continuously decreasing.

14 This term was coined by Hansmann (1980).

15 The best analysis of the problems with small decision-making is Hirsch (1977).

16 McLean (1987: Chapter 8) considers Condorcet's and Borda's recommendations side-by-side. The procedures themselves are described in Chapter 7 below.

3 THE EVOLUTION OF THE PARLIAMENTARY ELECTORAL SYSTEM

1 Pliny's letter to Titus Aristo in which the problem of voting procedures was outlined was translated into English in 1752. McLean (1989) has pointed out that there was some knowledge in the late medieval period of aspects of voting procedures. Ramon Lull (1235–1315) proposed choice by pairwise comparison, and Nicholas Cusanus (c. 1401–64) proposed rank-order voting.

2 It is interesting to note that Trinity College, Dublin is represented in the Senate of the Irish Republic today; the voters are the graduates of the university.

3 One consequence with the union with Scotland is worth noting. The Scottish burghs were too numerous to be granted even one MP each, so they were grouped together. This resulted in a two-stage election. Burgh councils would each elect a delegate, and the delegates would then meet to elect the MP. This system of election ended after 1832, although the grouping of Scottish burghs together in elections remained, and five still survived in 1945.

4 An argument attributed to Dilke by Blewett (1965: 31).

5 'In the extreme case of the South, the result was that by the mid-1920s presidential turnout had declined to about 18 per cent of the potential electorate.... Participation fell in the North and West as well, but very unevenly' (Burnham 1982: 139). On the factors which produce low voter turnout in the United States, see also Piven and Cloward (1988 and 1989).

6 An account of the different kinds of typologies is presented in Blais (1988).

7 Although they occur very rarely, tied elections are not unknown. A few years ago one of the authors was a resident in a ward where the district council election resulted in a tie; the contest was then decided on the toss of a coin.

8 Consequently, there may have to be many rounds of balloting in such elections. This seems to be usual in voting for a Pope, and the Democrats in 1924 had 103 rounds of balloting before agreeing on a candidate.

4 ELECTORAL SYSTEMS AND DEMOCRACY

1 The literature on democracy is so enormous that only a small section can be mentioned here. Two useful conceptual explorations are Lively (1975) and Arblaster (1987). Treatments of democratic theory which will lead to the wider literature are: Dahl (1979); Held (1987); Bobbio (1987); and Holden (1988).

2 'Positive' here means 'intended to provide an accurate definition of observed phenomena'.

3 This means only that we need to take account of a wide range of relevant features. It does not commit us to the view that what 'democracy' means is merely a matter of opinion.

4 During this century, there have been two unusual cases following an election when the leader of the largest party did not form the government. In 1918, the Prime Minister, Lloyd George, remained in office as head of a coalition government, even though his Coalition Unionist allies won enough seats to have formed a majority government by themselves. In the 1923 election, the Conservative government lost its overall majority and remained in office as the largest party until Parliament met; when it did so, the government was defeated immediately, and the leader of the Labour party formed a minority government. In addition, it is worth noting that in the December 1910 election, the two largest parties obtained the same number of seats, but it was clear that only the Liberals could obtain the necessary support of the Irish Nationalists.

5 Birch (1972) provides a good introduction to the complexities of the idea of representation.

6 This concept was introduced above, p. 57.

7 Obvious examples are: the relation between individual interests and the public interest; the nature of market outcomes in relation to individual

market decisions; the explanation of why an individual's preferences in collective decision-making differ from his or her preferences in isolation.

8 Of course, even a direct democracy using a voting system may encounter problems with cyclical patterns of preferences. See above, pp. 40–1.

9 The two most recent instances of this are: (1) 1940, when Neville Chamberlain resigned as Prime Minister after a vote of confidence in the Commons demonstrated that support for him had declined; and (2) 1979, when the minority Labour government was defeated in the Commons, thereby precipitating a general election.

10 Once again, we must bear in mind the problems of cycling and other constraints on the aggregation of preferences which will exist even in a direct democracy.

5   SECRET AND OPEN VOTING

1 A helpful and judicious review of Mill's theory of representative government is Thompson (1976).

2 Mill alludes to this episode briefly in his *Autobiography* (1971: 169). His essay *The Subjection of Women* (1983) is also important.

3 In Anthony Downs' book *An Economic Theory of Democracy* (1957: 7) a curious distinction is made about politically relevant aspects of a voter's utility schedule: 'Let us assume a certain man prefers party A for political reasons, but his wife has a tantrum whenever he fails to vote for party B. It is perfectly rational *personally* for this man to vote for party B if preventing his wife's tantrums is more important to him than having A win instead of B. Nevertheless, in our model such behavior is considered irrational because it employs a political device for a nonpolitical purpose.'

4 See above, p. 55.

5 Cf., e.g., Grimsley (1973: 115–19).

6 An interesting study of postal and workplace voting by trade union members (on the issue of unions' political funds) is Blackwell and Terry (1987: 630). While workplace voting can obviously be secret, the circumstances of the ballot differ.

7 See above, p. 37.

8 The most common example of this is probably the practice amongst trade unions of holding meetings to decide on acceptance or rejection of wage-bargains. Local branches delegate a person to cast a vote or votes according to the branch's view of the offer.

9 A vigorous essay on bribery and intimidation, and a call for the secret ballot, is James E. Thorold Rogers' 'Bribery' in Guttsman (1967), a selection from essays first published in 1867.

10 Of course, what a person 'really prefers' can easily become entangled with a view about what he or she *should* prefer.

11 That is, in an economic theory of democracy which focuses on the voter's expected utility from a party in government, the manifesto proclaims policy which will both benefit and disbenefit any one voter. In this sense the party is striking a bargain by making offers; it is, of course, the voter who usually has to look for the costs in terms of his or her utility.

6 THE TERRITORIAL DIMENSIONS OF ELECTIONS

1 It has been argued by some people that Richard Nixon actually received more votes than John Kennedy in 1960, but that voting fraud enabled Kennedy to appear to have a plurality in the popular vote. Kennedy won a majority of the Electoral College votes.

2 For a discussion of arguments about functional representation in the British state, see Birch (1964: 108–10).

3 Of course, territorial representation does not ensure the representation of more than one party in a legislature. One of the most astonishing examples of non-representation occurred in the Canadian province of New Brunswick in 1987. The governing Conservative party called an election at which the Liberal party won every seat.

4 Parties which draw on the support of geographically concentrated sub-groups in a society may be able to secure representation in smaller constituencies but not larger ones. For example, Plaid Cymru would probably not have any MPs if the House of Commons was reduced in size from 650 to, say, 325 constituencies because the total level of support they enjoy is concentrated but proportionately insufficient.

5 On the turnout rates of various liberal democracies, see Burnham (1987: Table 5.1).

6 For example, in the 1989 Irish general election the ruling Fianna Fail party suffered a proportionately greater loss in Parliamentary seats than in votes.

7 See also Taylor and Gudgin (1976).

8 The Labour party appears to be concerned to increase the representation of women in the Shadow Cabinet. Of course, there is a difference between increasing the influence of current women MPs and increasing the number of women in Parliament.

9 In Canada a party leader does have the power to remove a candidate nominated by a riding, but this power has been used only twice in fifteen years: it would create severe intra-party tensions if used more frequently.

10 In the United States special elections are always used to fill vacancies in the House of Representatives, but in the Senate a rather different practice is used. Because of the cost of holding a statewide election, a vacancy in the Senate is first filled through appointment by the state's Governor. An election for the unexpired period of the Senate term is then held at the same time as the next general election for House seats – the November of the next even-numbered year.

11 Another, more recent, example is that of the Vale of Glamorgan by-election in 1989, where the strength of one opposition party in the constituency (the Labour party in this case) resulted in its consolidating the votes of most 'oppositions'. The result was Labour's biggest by-election victory in a previously Conservative-held seat since 1935.

12 In Canada the governing party has more control than its counterpart in Britain because it can delay calling a by-election for longer and it also calls by-elections in seats previously held by other parties. In 1978 Prime Minister Trudeau called fifteen by-elections (representing 5 per cent of House seats) on the same day (Franks 1987: 61).

13 The plausibility of the 'mandate doctrine' in general was discussed in Chapter 4.

14 There is evidence that a fairly large minority of Scottish residents are not paying the tax, but it is not clear how many of them are merely 'tax-avoiders' rather than practitioners of civil disobedience.

15 Data gathered by Rush (1969) in the 1960s indicated that less than a quarter of candidates in winnable seats had direct links with their constituencies before being selected by their parties.

7   AGGREGATING VOTES: RIVAL SYSTEMS

1 An interesting study which blends the two approaches in slightly different measure is Bogdanor (1984).

2 See above, pp. 14–15.

3 See above, pp. 39–40.

4 A highly controversial treatment of abstentions occurred in a ballot conducted amongst council house tenants in Torbay. Tenants were asked to vote on changing their landlord, and an abstention was to be counted as a vote in favour of change. On this basis, it was claimed that a majority favoured change, a view that is defensible only if it is assumed that everyone knew the assumptions under which the ballot was conducted and had a reasonable and relatively costless opportunity to vote. *The Independent*, 21st November 1988.

5 See above, pp. 59–60.

6 See above, p. 6.

7 Kenneth Arrow put forward his theorem in 1951, and helpful discussions may be found in McLean (1987) and Colman (1982).

8 We are grateful to Iain McLean for drawing our attention to the discussion in Black (1958: 232–3).

9 Gibbard (1973) shows the generality of vulnerability.

10 See above, pp. 100–101.

11 There has been a considerable debate about the rationality of any particular voter troubling to cast his ballot: Barry (1970: 13–46) and McLean (1987: 45–9) take up themes from Downs (1957) and subsequent commentators.

12 See the table produced by Rose (1984) cited by Guntner (1989: 841).

13 Rawls (1972) proposed that just principles are those that rational and free persons would agree to in a position of initial equality. This equality could be hypothesized by placing the contractors behind a 'veil of ignorance' which would hide from them knowledge of their tastes, talents and so on. Each person, it was claimed, would be concerned not only with equal liberty but also to make the position of the worst-off person in society as good as possible: for each might turn out to be that worst-off person when the veil of ignorance was lifted.

14 See above, pp. 87–91.

References

Arblaster, Anthony (1987) *Democracy* Milton Keynes: Open University Press.

Arrow, Kenneth J. (1951) *Social Choice and Individual Values* New York: Wiley.

Barry, Brian (1970) *Sociologists, Economists and Democracy* Chicago: University of Chicago Press.

Barry, Brian (1980) 'Is it Better to be Powerful or Lucky?' Parts I and II, Political Studies 28: 183–94 and 338–52.

Beer, Samuel H. (1969) *Modern British Politics* London: Faber and Faber.

Birch, A.H. (1964) *Representative and Responsible Government* London: Allen and Unwin.

Birch, A.H. (1972) *Representation* London: Macmillan.

Black, Duncan (1958) *The Theory of Committees and Elections* Cambridge: Cambridge University Press.

Blackwell, Richard and Terry, Michael (1987) 'Analyzing the Political Fund Ballots: A Remarkable Victory or the Triumph of the Status Quo?', *Political Studies* 35: 623–42.

Blais, André (1988) 'The Classification of Electoral Systems', *European Journal of Political Research* 16: 99–110.

Blewett, Neal (1965) 'The Franchise in the United Kingdom 1885–1918', *Past and Present* 32: 27–56.

Bobbio, N. (1987) *The Future of Democracy* Cambridge: Polity Press.

Bogdanor, Vernon (1984) *What is Proportional Representation?* Oxford: Martin Robertson.

Brams, Steven J. (1976) *Paradoxes in Politics* New York: Free Press.

Brams, Steven J. and Fishburn P.C. (1978) 'Approval Voting', *American Political Science Review* 72: 831–47.

Burnham, Walter Dean (1982) 'The Appearance and Disappearance of the American Voter' in W.D. Burnham (ed.) *The Current Crisis in American Politics* Oxford and New York: Oxford University Press.

Burnham, Walter Dean (1987) 'The Turnout Problem' in A. James Reichley (ed.) *Elections American Style* Washington, DC: Brookings Institute.

Butler, David (1963) *The Electoral System in Britain Since 1918* 2nd Edition, Oxford: Clarendon Press.

Cain, Bruce E., Ferejohn, John A. and Fiorina, Morris P. (1983) 'The Constituency Component: A Comparison of Service in Great Britain and the United States', *Comparative Political Studies* 16: 67–91.

Cairns, Alan C. and Wong, Daniel (1985) 'Socialism, Federalism and the B.C. Party Systems, 1933–1983' in Hugh G. Thorburn (ed.) *Party Politics in Canada* 5th Edition, Scarborough, Ont.: Prentice Hall.

Cole, G.D.H. (1920) *Social Theory* London: Methuen.

Colman, Andrew (1982) *Game Theory and Experimental Games* Oxford: Pergamon.

Dahl, Robert A. (1989) *Democracy and its Critics* New Haven, CT: Yale University Press.

Dearlove, John and Saunders, Peter (1984) *Introduction to British Politics* Cambridge: Polity Press.

Downs, Anthony (1957) *An Economic Theory of Democracy* New York: Harper and Row.

Dummett, Michael (1984) *Voting Procedures* Oxford: Clarendon Press.

Duverger, Maurice (1954) *Political Parties* London: Methuen.

Ensor, R.C.K. (1936) *England 1870–1914* Oxford: Clarendon Press.

Franks, C.E.S. (1987) *The Parliament of Canada* Toronto: University of Toronto Press.

Friedrich, C.J. (1937) *Constitutional Government and Democracy* New York: Harper and Row.

Gibbard, A. (1973) 'Manipulation of Voting Schemes: A General Result', *Econometrica* 41: 587–601.

Goodwin, Barbara (1984) 'Justice and the Lottery', *Political Studies* 32: 190–202.

Grimsley, Ronald (1973) *The Philosophy of Rousseau* Oxford: Oxford University Press.

Gunther, Richard (1989) 'Electoral Laws, Party Systems and Elites: The Case of Spain', *American Political Science Review* 83: 835–58.

Guttsman, W.L. (ed.) (1967) *A Plea for Democracy* London: MacGibbon and Kee.

Hansmann, Henry (1980) 'The Role of Non-profit Enterprise', *Yale Law Journal* 89: 835–901.

Held, David (1987) *Models of Democracy* Oxford: Polity.

Hirsch, Fred (1977) *Social Limits to Growth* London: Routledge and Kegan Paul.

Hobbes, Thomas (n.d.) *Leviathan* (ed. Michael Oakeshott) Oxford: Basil Blackwell.

Holden, Barry (1988) *Understanding Liberal Democracy* Deddington: Philip Allan.

Johnston, R.J. (1983) 'Texts, Actors and Higher Managers: Judges, Bureaucrats and the Political Organization of Space', *Political Geography Quarterly* 2: 3–19.

Jones, Peter (1988) 'Intense Preferences, Strong Beliefs and Democratic Decision Making', *Political Studies* 36: 7–29.

Keir, David Lindsay (1966) *The Constitutional History of Modern Britain Since 1945* 8th Edition, London: Adam and Charles Black.

Lasswell, Harold (1951) *Politics: Who Gets What, When, and How?* New York: Free Press.

Lipset, Seymour Martin and Rokkan, Stein (eds) (1967) *Party Systems and Voter Alignments*, New York: Collier Macmillan.

Lively, Jack (1975) *Democracy* Oxford: Basil Blackwell.

Lively, Jack, and Rees, John (1978) *Utilitarian Logic and Politics* Oxford: Clarendon Press.
Lovenduski, Joni (1986) *Women and European Politics* Brighton: Wheatsheaf.
Lovenduski, Joni (1990) 'Feminism and West European Politics: An Overview' in D.W. Urwin and W.E. Paterson (eds) *Politics in Western Europe Today* London: Longman.
Mackintosh, John (1967) 'Scottish Nationalism', *Political Quarterly* 38: 389–402.
McLean, Iain (1987) *Public Choice* Oxford: Basil Blackwell.
McLean, Iain (1990) 'The Borda and Condorcet Principles: Three Medieval Applications', *Social Choice and Welfare* 7: 99–108.
May, John D. (1978) 'Defining Democracy: A Bid for Coherence and Consensus', *Political Studies* 26: 1–14.
Mill, John Stuart (1910) *Utilitarianism, Liberty and Representative Government* London: Dent.
Mill, John Stuart (1971) *Autobiography* (ed. Jack Stillinger) Oxford: Oxford University Press.
Mill, John Stuart (1983) *The Subjection of Women* (published with Harriet Taylor Mill, *The Enfranchisement of Women*) London: Virago.
Mueller, Dennis C. (1979) *Public Choice* Cambridge: Cambridge University Press.
Muir, Richard and Paddison, Ronan (1981) *Politics, Geography and Behaviour* London and New York: Methuen.
O'Leary, Cornelius (1962) *The Elimination of Corrupt Practices in British Elections, 1868–1911* Oxford: Clarendon Press.
Olson, Mancur (1965) *The Logic of Collective Action*, Cambridge, MA.: Harvard University Press.
Piven, Frances Fox and Cloward, Richard A. (1988) *Why Americans Don't Vote* New York: Pantheon.
Piven, Frances Fox and Cloward, Richard A. (1989) 'Government Statistics and Conflicting Explanations of Nonvoting', *PS* 22: 580–8.
Prewitt, Kenneth (1970) 'Political Ambitions, Volunteerism and Electoral Accountability', *American Political Science Review* 64: 5–17.
Prewitt, Kenneth and Nowlin, William (1969) 'Political Ambitions and the Behavior of Incumbent Politicians', *Western Political Quarterly* 22: 298–308.
Rae, Douglas (1971) *The Political Consequences of Electoral Laws* Revised Edition, New Haven, CT: Yale University Press.
Rawls, John (1972) *A Theory of Justice* Oxford: Clarendon Press.
Riker, William (1986) *The Art of Political Manipulation* New Haven, CT and London: Yale University Press.
Riley, Patrick (1986) *The General Will Before Rousseau* Princeton, NJ: Princeton University Press.
Rose, Richard (1982) *Understanding the United Kingdom* London: Longman.
Rose, Richard (1984) 'Electoral Systems: A Question of Degree or Principle?' in Arend Lijphart and Bernard Grofman (eds) *Choosing an Electoral System* New York: Praeger.
Rousseau, J-J. (1913) *The Social Contract and Discourses* (ed. G.D.H. Cole) London: Dent.
Rush, Michael (1969) *The Selection of Parliamentary Candidates* London: Nelson.
Schumpeter, Joseph A. (1967) 'Two Concepts of Democracy' in Anthony

Quinton (ed.) *Political Philosophy* Oxford: Oxford University Press, pp. 153–88.

Searing, Donald D. (1985) 'The Role of the Good Constituency Member and the Practice of Representation in Great Britain', *Journal of Politics* 47: 348–91.

Seymour, Charles (1915) *Electoral Reform in England and Wales* New Haven, CT: Yale University Press.

Sugden, Robert (1981) *The Political Economy of Public Choice* Oxford: Martin Robertson.

Taylor, P.J. and Gudgin, G. (1976) 'The Myth of Non-Partisan Cartography: A Study of Electoral Biases in the English Boundary Commissions', *Urban Studies* 13: 13–25.

Thompson, Dennis F. (1976) *John Stuart Mill and Representative Government* Princeton, NJ: Princeton University Press.

Tufte, Edward (1978) *Political Control of the Economy* Princeton, NJ: Princeton University Press.

Urwin, Derek (1977) *Electoral Systems* Bergen: Institute for Sociology and Political Sciences.

Urwin, Derek (1987a) 'Choosing Representatives: Majority Electoral Systems', *Social Studies Review* 3 (March): 23–30.

Urwin, Derek (1987b) 'Electing Representatives: Proportional Systems', *Social Studies Review* 3 (May): 1–12.

Ware, Alan (1985) *The Breakdown of Democratic Party Organization, 1940–1980* Oxford: Clarendon Press.

Wood, David M. (1987) 'The Conservative Member of Parliament as Lobbyist for Constituency Economic Interests', *Political Studies* 35: 393–409.

Index